YOUR FIRST
ATLANTIC
CROSSING

Other Titles of Interest

The Atlantic Crossing Guide edited by Anne Hammick
ISBN 0-7136-4839-2
A standard reference book for anyone contemplating crossing the Atlantic. It helps you to plan your crossing giving information including equipping your boat, route planning, provisioning, navigation and port details.

Atlantic Pilot Atlas by James Clarke
ISBN 0-7136-4554-77
A complete guide to the weather of the north and south Atlantic, the Mediterranean and the Caribbean through 40 specially drawn charts which detail wind, current and sea conditions.

The Voyagers Handbook by Beth A Leonard
ISBN 0-736-4937-2
An invaluable handbook for anyone contemplating an extended cruise. It is packed with information on techniques and gear as well as practical advice on many aspects of cruising.

Oean Cruising on a Budget by Anne Hammick
ISBN 0-736-4069-3
An essential guide for all those planning a blue water cruise whether on a budget or not. It gives advice on choosing a boat and equipment. Provisioning, safety, watchkeeping and many other topics.

Handbook of Offshore Cruising by Jim Howard
ISBN 0-7136-4044-8
Jim Howard has been cruising the oceans of the world for some twenty years, and in this book shows how the dream of offshore cruising can become a reality.

Using PCs on Board by Robert Buttress & Tim Thornton
ISBN 0-7136-5289-6
All the information you need to set yourself up with with a computer on your boat including installing and looking after a PC on board, choosing software, power supplies, interfacing and upgrading.

Saga of a Wayward Sailor by Tristan Jones
ISBN 0-7136-4277-7
Tristan sails the Baltic Sea, the English Channel, the Bay of Biscay and the Atlantic Ocean and the inland waterways of Weatern Europe.

There be no Dragons by Reese Palley
ISBN 0-7136-4713-2
How to cross a big ocean in a small yacht – this book looks at the equipment and skills that a new sailor will need to come safely to port.

YOUR FIRST ATLANTIC CROSSING

A planning guide for passage makers

Les Weatheritt

ADLARD COLES NAUTICAL
London

*Special thanks to the crew for coming with me
and to Annabel and Ronnie for helping me tell the story.*

Published 2000 by Adlard Coles Nautical
an imprint of A & C Black (Publishers) Ltd
35 Bedford Row, London WC1R 4JH
www.adlardcoles.co.uk

Copyright © Les Weatheritt 2000

Illustrations by Charles Shearer
Hull and rigging drawings by Ronnie Maclellan
All photographs by the crew

ISBN 0-7136-5102–4

A CIP catalogue record for this book is available from the British Library.

Note: While all reasonable care has been taken in the publication of this
book, the publisher takes no responsibility for the use of the methods,
products or personal opinions described in the book.

Typeset in 11 on 13pt Bembo
Printed and bound in Great Britain by The Cromwell Press,
Trowbridge, Wiltshire

Contents

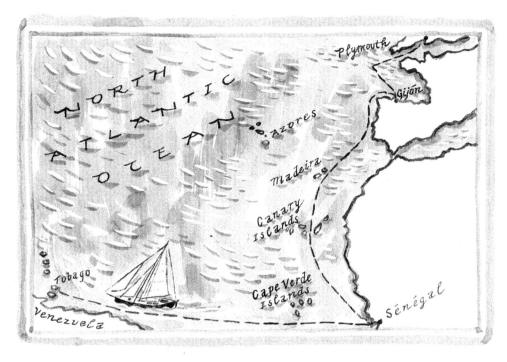

Our version of the 'Milk Run'.

Getting past go

♦ *Details make you safer and increase your confidence.*
♦ *This Atlantic crossing is one of the safest ocean routes, but still different from the sailing you may have done before.*
♦ *There is a lot of technical advice and personal anecdotes available about crossing the Atlantic, but nothing that 'holds your hand' on a first crossing. This book addresses your emotional and personal needs, as well as tackling the technical.*
♦ *People who have made the crossing have learnt a lot and will share it with you when you meet them. By then it will be too late. Read this book first.*
♦ *This book is for ordinary people rather than wacky heroes.*

What I really want to know. . .

What I really wanted to know before I set out to cross the Atlantic Ocean was whether I could survive. I mean, what is the point if you don't? That simple little question is a tricky one to get right. A lot of careful planning can help bolster confidence that setting off will eventually be followed by arrival. Good research on things like provisions and places on the way will help bring a wonderful anticipatory feeling that the trip might even be a lot of fun. Avoiding some topics of research, such as the fairly obvious difficulties a singlehanded sailor might have in performing open-heart surgery in a gale without his reading glasses, will also raise the level of confidence, but in what a mathematician might call a 'non-negative' way. That is, not doing that sort of research won't actually make you happier. Doing it will certainly depress the hell out of you.

I was forty-seven and a half, my crew were in their twenties, and our mental ages were not something to brag about. We were old enough to know better, immature enough not to, daft enough to give it a shot, and smart enough to have fun, fun, fun on our ocean crossing.

One particular route across the Atlantic is known as the Milk Run, because it is about as easy as any ocean sailing passage can be. Now that I've done it I think it probably is, but I wasn't so sure back then. I mean, how do you feel to be 2000 miles offshore in a boat that is a lot smaller than the last wave that just went past, and with another 1000 miles to go before you sight land? I know people who get anxious about crossing the North Sea, and that only takes 24 hours in anything more than a dead calm. I don't just *know* wimps like that: I'm one of them. So you can begin to appreciate how much reassurance I felt I needed before I set out on my own Atlantic crossing.

1

The thing is that you need this reassurance before you can really bring yourself to get down to the committed planning of the trip, but it is only when you lose yourself in the planning and the practicalities that you begin to feel that you can manage this wonderful adventure. To begin with, you feel less of a fool telling other people about your intentions if you have a clear idea of how far the crossing is and how long it will take to get to the other side. If, on top of that, you can talk about how to bake bread and how many showers will be allowed from *x* number of gallons of water carried in at least two tanks, then you will save yourself ego-injury and loss of confidence by the Machiavellian tactic of boring your friends out of any desire to ask difficult questions about the trip.

About 90 per cent of my worries came from the sailing heroes. You know who I mean. Fearless sailors inclined to mishap. They write all the good books. Ripping yarns, but frightening when you come to cast off from the pontoon. Where was the book by a sailing rabbit, who didn't spit in the eye of the storm, laugh scornfully at the iron-bound lee shore or whiplash the inadequates who dared call themselves crew? I never found it.

You will need to read many books before setting out on an Atlantic crossing. You may read them for fun, long before the seed germinates or the plans start to be made. You may already be well into the Hiscocks and the Smeetons, the Coles and the O'Briens, the Chichesters and Tilmans, and Slocum of course (see Appendix 2). My little book cannot compete with these giants of blue water sailing. But then, I'm not one of those giants and my book isn't being written for people like them. It's being written for you.

Petronella takes care of herself as usual, and we three pose in mid ocean.

I read many books, for entertainment and enlightenment. Somehow something was missing. I knew that then. I know it even more now, having made the journey. None of those books quite told the journey as it panned out. First, take the physical conditions such as the weather, for example. It was there on the page, but somehow the weather we had was never quite as I had expected. There are good reasons for that and I can work them out now that I have made the trip, but that didn't help me then to put orders of magnitude on what fears were justified and what ones were not. Second, take the social conditions of the trip. The issues of selecting and living with crew were barely covered, or at least not in any way that lived up to the reality as we experienced it. Yet this is pivotal to the sailing adventure. Get it right and you can have the perfect crossing, regardless of much else. Get it wrong, and life in paradise will be hell.

I needed a first book to introduce me to the facts, fears and fun of an ocean journey. To see not only how other beginners coped, but also what they learnt from the experienced sailors they met. To lead me to more reading with more understanding. To encourage me to just go. Since I didn't find one, I had to write one.

What I really missed from my reading before I set off was the story of an ordinary Joe doing what I was planning to do. I know now, of course, that the best way to hear the stories of ordinary Joes is to meet them in the outer harbours of places like Falmouth or Bayona or Funchal or Arguiniguin. It is easy to meet these long-distance cruising people when you are on a long-distance cruising yacht of your own. And it is easier to bump into these people the farther south you go. But by then you are on your way, past the point where you still need the gentle push that this book will give you.

This book covers my experience in setting out and completing an Atlantic crossing, but it is also a book for any ocean crossing; the broad points apply and the lessons we learnt are universal.

A day in the life . . . despite everything, it's fun

Listen. Whatever else happened out there as we went across the ocean, we had a great time. I learnt two lessons that I could only have learnt on that trip, and which I think should be passed on in the clearest terms to all those reading this book. The first was that sailing to the south is like no sailing you will ever experience in northern waters. Sailing changes in nature as the sun shines hotter, as the skies stay bluer and the water temperature rises. The second lesson is not so enjoyable. And I am not going to tell you what it is just yet. For the time being, just sit back and let your imagination take over.

We came out of the north with winter on our tail and summer in our eyes. Each passage we made brought warmer and drier air. We were the lotus eaters on our small sturdy yacht. We took our punishment in Biscay and sang at the gales. We rode a steady north wind all the way from Spain to Madeira. From Madeira we ghosted our way to the lonely Salvagen Islands and then tore south to the Canaries on a fine beam reach.

We came up on Tenerife island in silver moonlight as bright as day. The huge moon seemed to fill half the cloudless sky. When the moon went down we were sailing south-west in falling winds, parallel to the northern coast of Tenerife about 20 miles off, on course for the smaller island of Gomera. The highest mountain of Spain took on a blackish outline that gradually softened and warmed as the sun rose to port. Then as we slipped down the channel between Tenerife and Gomera, we found both were fading from sight as the air filled with fine Saharan dust.

Sailing in the south is a different, more sensual experience. Some might say easier. By the time you get that far, you are well on the way to being masters of the conditions.

The south wind came barrelling out from between the two islands, pushing steep short seas ahead of it and hitting us at force 6 to 7. The boat, with full sail set, slammed over from a near dead run to a hard beat and we were off, hammering in towards Tenerife until that rocky shore was unpleasantly close. So we tacked away from Tenerife towards the backside of Gomera, quite unable to make our planned harbour to the south. We would seek shelter in the lee of Gomera some 20 miles away.

Julia and I were in the cockpit, Julia on the tiller holding the boat hard on the wind while trying to dodge the worst of the breaking waves. The channel between

Julia and I were in the cockpit, with Julia on the tiller holding the boat hard on the wind.

the islands was row after row of white crests. *Petronella* stood on her ear like never before. The starboard deck was under water, and water stood on the lee-side locker seat. We stood on the lee-side locker edge. Hard, solid water was flung at us, which then curved and bounced around to find its way down below. For the first time since England we had sea water on the galley floor and running into the bilges. The spray blotted out my sunglasses. Our shorts and tee-shirts were clinging wet. Yet this was too much fun to stop. We whooped and roared and hung on to full sail for three hours until we were at last too cold to want more spray and still too far from the lee of Gomera. I went forward and did what I could have done at any moment during the last three hours: I double reefed the main and dropped the stay-sail. It took me about ten minutes. The motion eased immediately. I got us some dry clothes. Within the hour, soft winds were taking us up to a small calm bay. Magnus came up from his sleep and would not believe our story. We could hardly believe he had slept.

It was dark when we anchored. We ran in as close to shore as we dared in the fading light and then out a smidgen to drop anchor in what we hoped was sand. Surf pounded on the stony beach but the wind was still southerly, from the land. On either side of the mile-wide bay stood small volcanic mountains. A valley ran up the centre of the bay to the higher mountains of the interior. The moon had not yet risen and all we saw were these peaks in outline, the white breaking surf and the lights of the few houses as they flickered on around the bay. No other boat was there. That was how we came to the Canaries. It was a typical day in our journey.

Of course, by now we were well into our adventure and had become masters of conditions like this.

Life on earth – not burning all your bridges

There are three essential thought processes to go through before you arrive at the practical stage of dealing with your need to retain life, love and livelihood back home. The first of these is the longest and most troublesome. It is also the most pointless. It should be short-circuited and binned as soon as possible. If you can, I see no need for the prospective Atlantic-crossing sailor to lose as much sleep over it as I did.

This first stage is when, with mental arithmetic, pencil and paper or computer spreadsheet, you create a balance sheet of financial and social income and expenditures to show what will be irretrievably lost or damaged by your irresponsible wish to interrupt the comfortable life you have spent so long building just so that you can indulge this antisocial fantasy to sail across an ocean. The best hours spent on this complicated and insoluble calculus come as you cruise the motorways at the wheel of your car, stare idly at your reflection in the window of a train, or contemplate the hot-water tap as you soak in the bath. The worst hours are those when your mind won't slow down to let you fall asleep, or you wake in the middle of the night with the hot flush of a new fear of failure.

Pencil and paper are not helpful in any real way at this stage. The fears that occupy you can't be added up. Filling in columns and rows on graph paper is displacement activity while you delay getting to the vital but brutal second stage. This second stage is that brief moment of total irrationality when you finally say, 'Oh sod it, I'm going.' There is no justification for your decision. No calculus to show its impact on your future. If you are lucky, this moment comes in a sudden blinding flash of inspiration, no more subject to analysis or reconsideration than any other half-cocked conversion. If you are unlucky, it comes after a long grinding period of vacillation when finally you can no longer bear the thought that you are more mouse than man, and you just jump.

Get it in perspective. You are not running away to be a sea-gypsy. It's just like an extended cruise. Therefore life back home must be maintained. Detailed planning is essential and will help you to make the emotional commitment to go. But you must make that commitment at some stage.

Now comes the third stage. In form it is very like the first stage, in that it involves the detailed construction of a social and financial balance sheet and many sleepless nights, but this stage is marked with purpose and deadlines. You are on your way now. It isn't just a matter of time. It's a matter of timing.

This adventure is not about burning all your bridges. Some of the most interesting questions faced by someone sailing a boat across an ocean are about the life they are leaving and how they will pick it up again. I mean, life at home may be getting you down just now, but it will have a new and rosy glow after six months or more on a small ocean-going boat.

The Atlantic circuit can, in theory, be done in a year and this is more or less what I had in mind. A trip spread over a year is, in many practical ways, similar to an extended cruise to faraway parts of Europe. You would probably sail out in one summer and return in the following one, leaving the boat to winter out there. Over these 12 months you would probably have two major disruptions of about four months each when you were away or occupied with boaty things. The point is, you haven't gone 'live-aboard'. You are on an extended sailing trip with all the domestic systems back home still to be maintained.

My planned Atlantic crossing was not much different from that. I was not running away to sea for ever. I just wanted to see if I could sail the ocean, and after that I would return to real life ashore. In its original form, I planned to sail down to the Canaries in late autumn, cross to the Caribbean at Christmas, and sail for home again in early summer. The weather determines this sort of timetable for a round trip, and I was happy to work within it. So I wasn't going to rent out my home. I wasn't going to give up work. I wasn't going to put family and friends on hold. Lots of other people I met were also treating their Atlantic crossing as an extended cruise. All of us, then, had to work out the most effective and least disruptive ways of leaving our affairs ticking over for a longer period than usual.

Detailed planning was, of course, the least part of getting comfortable with this intention. Much more significant was whether those loose ends could ever be picked up again or whether, despite all endeavours to the contrary, my bridges would be badly scorched, if not actually burnt. Like many people thinking of an Atlantic circuit, I have to earn my living. I have no inheritance, no private income, not even a win on the Grand National to sustain me. When I sail, my earnings cease. The same is not true of my expenditures. A little bit of me remains forever England, and it costs.

The things I had to deal with are probably not very different from yours. I needed to maintain a flat with a mortgage and a working and romantic relationship. A year playing at sailing was about all I could allow if I was not to let either the intellectual stimulus of work or the essential contacts pass me by. I carefully worked out the stages of my Atlantic circuit to see where I could take time out from sailing to come back and revive the life I had left behind. The heart of my concern was financial. I am a freelance research economist, and I typically work on projects lasting from two to six months. My ideal would be to slot my trip into the closing stages of one project and the opening round of another when the work is less concentrated. If I was lucky,

This is not about burning your bridges.

my time without paid work would not be so long that the inescapable bills of shore life bankrupted me. If I had to break my trip to do work, well, at least it would pay the airfares back from Spain or Madeira or wherever. And any time spent back in the UK on work would also help keep up my social life. As, of course, would having friends come out to sail with me.

As a freelance consultant I have, in theory, the flexibility to find time for long breaks within my pattern of work. In practice, this never happens. Freelancing may be a quantum of personal freedom greater than conventional employment, but for most of the time the effective freedom is to exploit yourself on behalf of clients who back-slappingly envy your autonomy while taking twice as much time in holidays as you dare. I also have responsibilities to my colleagues in our tiny consultancy, to pull my weight and help keep the business flowing. The key part of my decision to go sailing was reaching an agreement with my partner on how this could be arranged and getting her enthusiastic support. Then, once I could talk about the trip as an event with a starting date, the natural momentum of the adventure took over, in part driven by other people's expectations. All sorts of people make allowances and contributions that smooth the way. Only my old friends, in those reflective conversations in front of strong drink and an evening fire, were able to remind me that this major step was no more than a natural consequence of all those working and lifestyle decisions I had stubbornly taken over the last decade. How easy life becomes.

What is out there? A breaking wave of fear

A philosopher might argue that fear of the unknown defines mankind. It probably defines all other life forms too, from amoeba to great white whale. It certainly defines those who go to sea in small boats, if they have any sense or finer feelings. Fear of the unknown is perfectly reasonable. Fear of the known is not to be despised either. Even those who have sailed a stretch of sea or ocean a hundred times can hardly claim to know it in any way that removes fear. The bigger the bit of water, the less you can know or predict what will happen while you are sailing on it. So don't let fear stop you from doing this, or any of the other worthwhile things you have in mind.

♦ Being afraid of undertaking this adventure is normal.
♦ There is no good reason to be more afraid as distance offshore increases.
♦ We didn't encounter the things that worried us.

What concerned me most before I set off, and ranks as a Class A Fear, was what conditions we would meet at sea and our probability of being overwhelmed by them. This is the mark of the practical sailor. Or the coward. Whichever, I knew that we were going to be a long way offshore and well outside the range of the lifeboat service, and that the ocean is as mean as the sea, but with a bigger and nastier attitude.

There have been times before this voyage when I have feared being wrecked. In storms on the, admittedly much smaller, North Sea and English Channel, I have been near to tears with frustration because the violent motion of the boat would not let me complete a simple task. If only the sea would be still for a minute I could use both hands to get the half-frayed end of that line through the block. If only the wind would stop screaming in my ears for 30 seconds I could think straight and work out how to get the bar-taut knotted sheets off the tangled jib. I have sailed in the rock-strewn tidal channels of Brittany in 100 metre visibility, desperate for a green light and have suddenly seen a line of white water dead ahead. I have plotted my way across river bars and felt that heart-stopping moment when the echo sounder shows zero and the following sea curls into a breaking crest and you are alone in a cruel place with nothing to expect but a jarring crash as 10 tons of boat drops its narrow keel onto rock-hard sand rising through receding water.

So none of that stuff bothered me very much. If I could get away with being an idiot around the European coast, I could manage it in other places too. What was new and all too unknown was what might happen 1000 miles off land. Surely the storms were bigger, lasted longer, brewed monster waves, and were relentlessly frequent. I know that the Admiralty plotting charts, showing in neat little diagrams all those weather observations that ships' captains have been wonderful enough to send in for the last few hundred years, do not lead to this conclusion. They show rather nice weather along the ocean route from the Canaries to the Caribbean, with most winds comfortably from the east and rarely over force 6. Well, those trusty old ships' captains are on rather large vessels and may not notice the gale-force wind that only blows for an hour or two. Well, I would notice it. Those 20 foot waves are no problem to the ocean tanker, but they are to me. Anyway, the past is not a certain guide to the future, as any dinosaur would tell you. Look at the greater incidence of hurricanes in the last decade. Or at least that is what it feels like ever since the trees in my street got blown down in 1987.

And if it isn't enough that commercial captains underestimate the tempests, what about the flotsam and jetsam they leave behind them? All those horror stories of 20 ton cargo containers falling off the deck. I don't want to frighten anyone, but a container is a big hard lump of steel for a sailing boat to hit at night. One full of ping-pong balls could be floating around the ocean for years knocking us sailors off like flies. Someone might like to work up an analysis of sinkings that attributes the loss of shipping in the Bermuda Triangle to some rogue ping-pong container trapped eternally in the currents there. Feel free. Borrow the idea. I don't feel possessive about it.

And it isn't just containers. One night, years ago, far offshore and storm-lashed in the treacherous Bristol Channel, my 24 footer and I sailed right up to a huge old concrete and steel thingy that was floating low in the water. I was lucky to see it as the last light of day drained from that ferocious sky. As I recall, the thingy had awesome spikey bits sticking out that would have holed us as soon as say 'Mayday, Mayday, Mayday'. I tried to report it on the VHF, but couldn't raise any interest. And then it floated away and I lost sight of it in the dark, never to see it again. But it was there. Honest. I mean, it was me who saw it.

And as for whales. This life force, so large and intelligent, just might want to take some revenge for your failure and mine to get the Russians and Japanese to join the international ban on commercial whaling. Such brainy beasts are hardly going to head-bang a 10,000 ton ship with sonar detectors and ready-primed explosive harpoons. Not likely. This marine Napoleon would rather find some little yacht carelessly bobbing up and down on the bright blue sea and give it such a slapping with its flukes *pour encourage les autres*.

And if these external sources of disaster were not enough, what if a seacock jammed and water flooded in as we slept? Of course, we would wake before this sank us, but with gallons of briny in the bilges our boat would sit so low in the water that some rogue wave would poop us and disable us so that the next monster would swamp us completely. And we would go down because the bilge strainer was blocked by some trashy paperback my crew had dropped as they fell asleep, all unaware of the tragic events about to unfold. No wonder I have trouble sleeping at night.

Honestly, a lot can frighten a sailor. I wanted to be told that none of this was going to happen to me, any more than I would fall overboard one dark night and watch *Petronella* sail on with my crew asleep or drunk and the self-steering soberly alert and steering us. All the world in its allotted place, apart from me.

The point of all this is that I discovered no evidence that these fears should grow in proportion to distance offshore or depth of sea under the hull. We didn't see a lot of this frightening stuff. We certainly suffered some stronger winds than the plotting charts would have us believe. We nearly got run down one night by a fish-ing boat when we were a few hundred miles offshore. We met a pod of killer whales that were reputedly intelligent enough to attack French yachts. We didn't see pirates, but we might have done. And I got rather worried when I thought we were going to be swamped on the bar of an African river before we started our Atlantic crossing. But when we surfed into Tobago our main concerns were those common to all travellers everywhere: Customs, Immigration, cold beer and clean sheets to sleep in.

The boat

- *Don't spend too much time thinking about 'the ideal boat'.*
- *Make the best of what you have.*
- *My boat wasn't perfect either!*
- *I learnt a lot from previous, shorter, journeys. It all helped with the ocean. You need to get the feel for your boat.*
- *Both monohulls and multihulls have advantages and disadvantages.*
- *Boats have character. Those with a smile make friends for you.*
- *Fit some fans. It's going to get hotter.*
- *Simplify everything for safety and efficiency, even if you have to dump the heirlooms.*

Built like a rock, so what if she sinks?

An adventure like this can get off to a bad start over the type of boat needed. I'm very pleased with my choice of boat, since I already owned her and didn't have to find another. My *Petronella* was not ideal, not by any means, but she was a good compromise. More to the point, I could easily have lost all momentum by trying to sell my old boat or gone broke raising the money for a new one. As we travelled south we came across all sorts of boats making this trip. There was so much variation that I began to think that it barely mattered what the boat was, just so long as it was well cared for and the crew were good enough.[1]

Petronella is 32 feet long, or more if you count the bowsprit and the steel bumpkin that carries her self-steering. She is a heavy-displacement C-Mist 32 double-ender loosely following the Colin Archer style, but designed by Samson Marine of Canada and built in Oban, Scotland, by her original owners. She was 16 years old when we set out from England for the Bay of Biscay.

Petronella has a ferro-cement hull and deck. I have lost count of the number of people who go all wide-eyed and innocent and tell me, 'But concrete doesn't float.' Some of them are standing on the deck at the time. Her construction gives me enormous confidence in her integrity and her ability to withstand some hard knocks. Years earlier, in a choppy Dutch river, I had watched helpless as a huge passing bow wave lifted my boat and dropped her onto the unforgiving end of a suddenly uncovered steel pile. It looked and sounded horrible. The hard-bitten friend sailing with me was near to tears, but all *Petronella* suffered was a scratch. I

---

[1] Crew is a word with many connotations. I mainly give it two meanings. Sometimes it means all of us on board, acting together as sailors. Us against the elements; equals with a shared purpose. Sometimes it means Magnus and Julia only, with me being the skipper. Them and Me. I hope you can always spot the difference.

Photographic proof that concrete yachts like Petronella *do float.*

have seen her bowsprit embarrass me by sneaking over the deck of a much larger wooden yacht and casually pulling the bolts of the guard rail stanchions through the timber deck. The owner should have been more grateful to discover that such vital safety gear was so flimsy. It would take Galileo and a very long lever arm to pull the bolts through the ferro deck on *Petronella*.

I rate ferro-cement as second only to steel for blue water sailing, and well ahead of plastic and wood. I am not even convinced that steel is better. I know that most of the sailing world begs to differ over the merits of ferro, and so be it. Most of these people have never lived with a ferro boat so they don't know the real qualities of the material. Much of the bad image of ferro comes from unfinished wrecks left rotting in the front gardens of amateurs who started building blue water 40 footers when they would have been better off with a reservoir dinghy. I knew *Petronella* was a good boat from the moment I saw her. The surveys and her performance have all confirmed this. The original builders of *Petronella* were short of money (like many other amateur builders), but not short of time, commitment or skills. They not only put together the steel cage that forms the skeleton of the hull and deck, but they also made many of the original fittings themselves. The home-made timber mast and its steel fittings have proved enormously strong. They built good and they built strong, these men of Oban. They also built heavy, and while I don't mind that, given the alternative, I have had to dump some of the original bits and pieces.

A material issue

Your choice of material is not just a matter of what is ideal for your sailing plans, but also what is available and at the price you can afford. Most modern yachts, and therefore most of those for sale, are glassfibre reinforced plastic (GRP). This is now the standard material for yacht building in the industrialised world. Wood is the older building material, and it seems that steel is often the traditional preferred material in places where wood has been historically in short supply. Aluminium alloy is the modern version of steel. Ferro-cement is a long-established shipbuilding material that suddenly seemed on the verge of making it into yacht construction sometime in the 1950s and 1970s.

All these materials have their benefits and their drawbacks. All have evolved, so that there are now many forms of construction for each of them. None of them are wonder materials, as might once have been claimed. There is no perfect boatbuilding material. There are good and bad points for each. You could confuse yourself to a standstill by trying to cope with all the books written on these materials. Instead, all you need to decide which material is for you is a fairly crude summary of these many points.

GRP is physically the weakest of the construction materials, and is regarded with suspicion by some deep-ocean sailors as the least likely to survive whale attacks or collision with big floating lumps of whatever, but GRP hulls at least have the integrity of being a single moulding, whereas most ocean-going wooden boats are planked and can leak worryingly in heavy weather. Wood also rots, suffers worms, and the wetness inside the wood can destroy the metal fastenings holding it together. Wood needs particular and, I think, difficult skills to maintain. People fall into one of two categories: wooden boat lovers and those who are not. If you are not one of the former, then don't even think about making this your choice for your ocean adventure. I myself am not a wooden-boat man.

GRP, once thought to be rot-proof, suffers boat pox. Osmosis pulls water past the protective surface of the gel coat and into the glassfibre. The hull gets heavy with moisture and the strength of the material is threatened. Repair is expensive. Many modern GRP boats are reckoned to suffer osmosis after five to ten years. The longer they are left in the water, the quicker they suffer; salinity affects the rate of osmosis. So GRP is not a wonder material. These points aside, as the best material for mass production these boats dominate the market and are probably the easiest to buy and re-sell.

Steel is immensely strong and more able to survive whale attack and occasional encounters with coral reefs. It is heavy, so steel yachts are seldom smaller than 30 feet. It is not a smooth material and welding leaves seams, so the hull finish is never perfect, even when filled. Steel lends itself to one-off designs and limited production rather than mass production but the material is cheap to buy, readily available and, since easily fabricated, labour skills are also cheap and can be found everywhere. The simplest form of steel construction is chine, where flat plates are welded together to make a hull with angled sections. There are those who love the slab-sidedness of chine. Oh well. To my eye, the more attractive construction is rolled plate, where the flat plates are rounded. More attractive, stronger – but expensive.

The properties of steel make it the natural choice for many long-distance yachts. The problem is that steel rusts and always will. This need not put you off. Bernard Moitessier discovered the secret of steel. Keep the water out and the paint on. All you have to do is live on the boat, as Moitessier did, and keep chipping the rust and painting the steel, as happens on well-run commercial ships. Other sailors I have met adopt a more cavalier approach and regard it as quite natural to let the stuff rot to a dangerous thinness, grind these bits out, and then weld in patches. For these people, all steel hulls are good buys, but some are more of a bargain than others. No hull is beyond saving even if it involves living in a boatyard for a year or two up to your pillowcase in shot blast and noxious acid fumes. That, frankly, is not the life for me.

Aluminium alloy was at one time the wonder material to replace steel because it didn't rust. But nature is not to be cheated so easily. Aluminium erodes by electrolysis, which is always a potential reaction in any salt solution. The sea is a battery, and electrolysis is unpredictable – also, it is often invisible and deadly. It can burn complete holes through alloy, so all fittings and fastenings have to be very carefully chosen. Metal-based antifouling can colander a hull. Alloy is more expensive to produce than steel and, with much more care needed in boat construction, it is not easy to repair in out-of-the-way places.

Stainless steel, by the way, is a bit like aluminium. It is a metal alloy capable of rapid rates of erosion through electrolysis. The higher the grade of marine stainless steel, the better the components have been mixed. Even so, local concentrations can't be ruled out and these, when they occur, cause the erosion. The natural process of erosion does not need your builder to make a bad choice of fittings and fastenings. A lump of stainless steel has all it needs within itself to start the rot. For this reason, stainless steel is dangerous below the waterline whether as a whole hull or as a single bolt. Apart from that, it is expensive.

Ferro is the least common and most ignored material. It became a popular material, especially in Australia and New Zealand, because it was cheap, required few skills, no expensive mass production mouldings, and could be built in a backyard. These were wonderful advantages for the home builder, but the average home builder is such a bodger that the material got a bad reputation. Many people were carried away by the thought that they could afford a 55 foot home-made ferro hull instead of a 35 foot factory-moulded GRP hull. They forgot that the hull is only about one-quarter the cost of the finished yacht, and that the cost of fittings goes up exponentially with size. They went bust trying to fit out the bigger hull. They also tended to build bigger hulls because, like steel, the material is heavy and most designs start at 30 feet. The physical advantages of ferro are its huge strength and its relative lack of maintenance. Ferro boats are also cheap to buy.

If you are thinking of buying a boat for this adventure, rather than using the one you have, give some thought to this. Any boat is easy to buy, so if you want a boat only for this adventure think about the selling that must come later. Markets prefer standard products and well-known makes are the most frequently traded. Such makes are therefore easiest to sell afterwards. However, you pay for this initially. The idiosyncratic oddities are the cheapest boats and, as such, give you the most for your money. In my case, I knew that the yacht market rated ferro as an oddity, which is why I got so much more ocean-going boat for my money. I simply could not have afforded a GRP yacht with anything like *Petronella*'s competence.

In case you are thinking of compromising seagoing qualities to increase second-hand trade-ability: Don't. It's your life, not your money, you should value most.

Petronella

My boat is also unusual in being a Colin Archer type. I love the double-ended shape. I hope that there is truth in the claim that this shape causes less disturbance to an overtaking sea, because *Petronella*'s usual speed means she gets more overtaking seas than the average cruiser.

Petronella is a beamy boat for her length, and deep, with plenty of headroom and a feeling of spaciousness. She has six berths, two being pilot berths in the saloon. This gives a crew of three or four more than enough space for gear, and plenty of choice about where people sleep. The pilot berths, though airless, give crew undisturbed sleep on night passages. Also, regardless of the tack, we always have two good berths on the lee side.

My lovely *Petronella* is a rather small and unsophisticated sailing boat. You may be comparing her unfavourably with the boat you currently own or covet. And so you should. No owner worth his or her salt should acknowledge that there is a better boat than theirs. Yet my little boat still took me across the Atlantic. That makes your own boat just as capable.

Two important reasons made *Petronella* right for me. You need to give thought to how they relate to your existing or intended yacht. First, she had the heavy displacement and huge hull strength that I wanted on an ocean voyage but, second, I could still sail her singlehanded.[1] Both of these things were essential to making me feel comfortable and in control of what I planned. Now, having crossed an ocean, I might revise my ideas on the ideal hull. I might well prefer to sacrifice displacement for speed and manoeuvrability, but I am not about to act on this. First, ideal boats don't exist; and second, if they do, then they are only ideal for one purpose. Sailing is about all sorts of different activities and many different purposes. You can't always be sailing in the single way that best suits your boat. I can't forever keep *Petronella* at sea to avoid the gut-ways of Essex or the canals of Holland.

I made many trips in *Petronella* before I felt I should cross the Atlantic. The point is that none of them were on the scale of an ocean crossing, and yet all of them contributed to making that crossing. *Petronella* has many features that make me curse and sweat. That reassuringly heavy displacement also makes her slow and uncomfortable in some seas. Coping with her adverse features has widened my skills as a sailor as well as my vocabulary. Above all, it has given me confidence that I know her limits. The cursed foibles of your own boat will have done the same for you, but I doubt you ever thought of them in this positive and forgiving way.

First on my list of things to curse is *Petronella's* handiness in tight corners. She doesn't have any. Her long keel, inefficient rudder and tiny engine make her less manoeuvrable than most modern yachts. Over time I have learnt how to handle her and turn these problems into benefits. I know now, for example, that by backing and filling, with forward and reverse gears and hardly bothering to touch the tiller, I can turn her almost in her own length on the engine alone. She has the weight and good manners to do this perfectly, so long as there is no rush. But go anywhere where there is another yacht and there will be a rush for something. As a result, I will do almost anything to avoid a marina and regard anchoring as the natural consequence of sailing. So I have learnt from experience the need for anchor watches; to suspect the competence of sailors whose boat seems to have dropped back over my anchor; and to cope with my anchor warp snapping in the middle of the night.

Second, *Petronella* is very slow when the wind is light. This has taught me patience, but not enough. What it *has* taught me in abundance is how she handles in different weather and sea conditions. I mean, she and I are out there so much longer than the other boats that we get to see things they don't. Yachts that can cross 70 miles of North Sea in daylight and Biscay in a weekend just don't get the sea time. Nor do they catch those wicked winds that lie outside the accurate first eight hours of a three-day weather forecast.

That is just a very small part of what *Petronella* has taught me as a sailor. Life might have been easier without these lessons, but they have all helped. Your own boat will have its own sweet ways, and coping with them will teach you things that others will not know so well. You will be an expert in some things, even if it is only in navigating with a chart strapped to the toilet seat. I have learnt to sail with, rather

---

[1] I don't mean I wanted to sail her singlehanded. I mean that it is best to regard a crew of two, three or four as serial singlehanders unless you can really cope with sleep deprivation.

16

than against, the character of my boat, and I hope she has learnt the same about me. Getting across the ocean is largely about how well you know your boat and how well she knows you.

One hull or two?

On my journey across the ocean I observed one aspect of hull design to be so life-threateningly important that I want to add my contribution to the debate. For this big adventure, do you choose mono- or multihull?

I met a man in Spain sailing a catamaran who rather amusingly insisted on calling all monohulls 'half-boats'. I have to say that the joke wore thin very quickly for us monohullers, but the point is that quite a lot of the people we met chose catamarans for their size and stability. Cats certainly have a wonderful deck area for the tropics and I have been very tempted to try one out. The problem is getting to the tropics in the first place. I am a cautious and fearful sailor and want nothing to do with a boat that might prefer to hang around upside down after it has capsized. I know that there are some very esoteric technical arguments about hull stability, and whether multihulls do or don't turn over, and stay that way, any more than monohulls do. You can find such arguments in more erudite books than this. My observations don't address the ultimate danger of capsize, because I never came across this. They address the more mundane issue of survival in a storm.

While we were struggling with the bad weather that hit us crossing Biscay, so was a 46 foot catamaran. We later met the couple and their three small children in the small harbour of Gigon, northern Spain, and compared notes. While *Petronella* lay hove-to, bouncing up and down but making no more than a couple of knots, the cat had run under bare poles for two days. They were not confident enough in the strength of the hull to heave-to, and to let the boat take the seas. Because we were hove-to for the worst of the windy bits, we knew that there had been a lull of several hours before a second, more violent, gale came through. We knew this because the lighter wind made us go on deck to raise more sail. The cat, running so fast before the wind, didn't know there had been two gales. Even in the lull they had plenty of wind and waves to keep them up there surfing. To them, the two gales just felt like one long blast.

We let the self-steering on *Petronella* handle the storm. Our friends on the cat had no choice but to hand-steer as they ran. Even under bare poles this light and easily driven hull sometimes surfed off waves at 10 knots, and at that speed you can't let the self-steering make even a little mistake on your behalf. The first broach would be the last.

Two things strike me about this. First, I would not like to keep a crew of two hand-steering for 48 hours in a gale.[1] For one thing, hand-steering isn't done well enough when the crew is exhausted. For another, steering downwind in big

---

[1] The moment comes when any boat is in survival conditions, and when hand-steering on a run for days on end may be the only recourse. But the point for any ocean-crosser is to push back survival conditions as far as possible and not to suffer them in a typical Biscay gale.

following seas is potentially fatal at night, when big rogue seas are invisible. Second, travelling at 10 knots rapidly eats into your sea room. One of my comforts in heavy old *Petronella* was that it would be a week before we hit France and surfed into the nearest bistro. At 10 knots it would have taken us less than two days.

I would gamble on a Biscay gale never lasting as long as a week. I wouldn't gamble on it lasting less than two days.

Get a boat with a smile

One final point on choice of boat. I have observed a strange thing never mentioned in scholarly handbooks on hull design. Some boats are more naturally sociable than others. *Petronella* oozes sociability in a way I had never realised before.

The social contact that *Petronella* encourages is, of course, with low-budget sailors, but these are often the most adventurous and have the most entertaining stories. I had long suspected we fitted this category (cheap, I mean, not adventurous), but it was confirmed one day in Spain. We had just anchored when a Frenchman on a nearby yacht leapt into his tatty, tiny dinghy and embarrassingly paddled straight for us in that peculiarly French way, sitting right in the bow and defying the sea to swamp him. He was a very sociable man and starved of company. He waved an arm to encompass the dozen yachts in the anchorage and said Gallic-ly, 'None of these people want to speak with me. I know never to go over to them, not even to give

Petronella *is a boat with a smile.*

them advice. But as soon as I saw your boat I knew you were like me and that I would be welcome here.'

We immediately did our best to stop behaving like po-faced English and got out that bottle of *entente cordial* we had been saving for just this occasion. This type of experience was repeated many times. The English singlehander in his plywood gaffer who rowed over to show us the best anchorage in Madeira. The New Zealanders in their farm-built boat who adopted my crew in Porto Santo. The penniless Irish couple on an old Channel racer leaking through its caulking who lent us charts in the Canaries. The whole fleet of French rust buckets anchored off Dakar, whose continuing stay in Senegal is a tribute to the severity of yacht certification back in mainland France, and who *ça va*-ed us with bottomless charm every day of our stay.

A friend of mine, watching *Petronella*'s slow but determined entry into a marina, described her low-slung, dark hull and Viking credentials as 'sinister'. For my part, I like to think she comes in with a big 'Hello!' on her face.

Fan fare

If your boat, like mine, was designed to be cosy in the north, it will be over-cosy in the heat of the south. But your ventilation system must also take account of those cheeky little ocean waves that want to hop on board with you, just when you thought the sea had gone all quiet.

Petronella's deck vents gave us all the air we needed in Biscay when we had the main hatch shut and the weather boards in. Travelling south, the good weather and fair wind let us keep the main hatch open, but once we left the Canaries we needed more ventilation. In Senegal, the daytime cabin temperature was 30°C and dropped to 25°C at night. Not a lot of difference. The only time we needed even a sheet for sleeping was between 3 am and 7 am.

Just when we needed maximum air flow we actually halved the capacity of our deck vents. We fixed netting over the ventilation holes to protect ourselves from the disease-carrying mosquitoes of Africa and the Caribbean. Of course, we could have taken this off whenever we went offshore, but we would only have had to put it back on later. Anyway, I am not sure that the deck vents did much for comfort in the hot south. Our main ventilation was through the open fore hatch and main hatch.

We only had our fore hatch open at sea when working or lounging up on the foredeck and were able to keep an eye on the waves. I had read stories of yachts swamped by freak waves that just kept coming and coming, and we were able to see at first hand how, even in settled conditions, the sea always had a rogue wave or two. So the fore hatch was almost always closed when sailing, but especially at night. When it wasn't, we got punished.

We only needed weather boards during gales, but often sailed with the main hatch closed to keep spray out. I was surprised that even when reaching in a force 4 and flattish sea we had water running on the sidedecks and occasional spray over the coachroof. In the trades the seas got up very quickly with the wind. A force 6 squall over a normal force 4 raised the waves from 6 or 8 feet up to 10 or 15 feet. Any wind from a slightly different direction brought instant confusion to the prevailing wave track. Even little ocean waves throw 4 foot spray when your boat tries to shoulder them aside at 6 knots. Nothing stayed dry on deck or in the companionway.

Log entry: a wet surprise
Easy progress tonight . . . an easterly 4 with seas to match. We roll, and the odd big wave rolls us a bit more. Water on the sidedecks. Nothing special. And then we heard The Big One. All of us, whether asleep or on watch, heard this one coming.
   The wave hit the hull just forward of the main hatch, climbed up onto the sidedeck and then kept coming until it was up over the coachroof and running a wall of water downhill towards the foredeck. Julia was sleeping with fore hatch open just a crack . . . the wave dropped in to join her. We bailed out a few gallons and dried the bedding in the hot morning sun.

Mechanical ventilation would have immensely improved comfort down below, just by moving the air. The simplest solution I saw was four little computer fans, one at each corner of the main cabin. They consume little power, are cheap to buy, readily available, reliable, and much quieter than car fans. Of course, prolonged use might take more electricity than our 20 watt solar panel allows. No matter. One panel is not enough.

Less is more

The smaller, more cramped and specialised your living space, the more you need to have the simplest, most efficient gear. Few living spaces are smaller, more cramped and more specialised than a small ocean-going yacht. Except perhaps a small ocean-going rowing boat. Simplicity means speed and safety in operation. Efficiency means the fewest limbs to make it work. Together these help achieve the near-impossible on a small sailing boat: comfort. The best changes are those that don't just do one more job, but make every previous job easier or better. Think about this as you cast an eye over the love of your (sailing) life.

   Start with the galley, the focus of life below decks. This must be practical in all conditions if life on board is to achieve any degree of comfort. I can make do with lying on the unswept floor slowly chewing a damp cracker for the first two days of most voyages, but after that I want fresh coffee and hot grub. The galley had better be up to it. Beware of any sailor who says, 'But we never cook at sea,' to excuse the lack of gimbals or handholds in their galley. Do they get their take-aways helicoptered in?

   The cook needs two working hands at all times and should never have to commit one to remaining upright. I watched a friend of mine on a classic blue water yacht backflip across the galley and into the navigatorium while holding a carving knife, all for lack of well-placed supports at the sink. He was lucky and did not frighten me too badly. There is no point-of-sailing on the various sailing legs on this ocean journey from Europe to Paradise where the boat isn't defying the cook to fall over. Sailing down Channel: tack, tack and tack. Crossing Biscay: heeled 20 degrees. Spain to Africa: slopping around in beam seas. Trade winds: more slopping around, and then the unlooked-for joy of rhythmic rolling. The first item of safety in our galley is a simple webbing strap on a hook. In use, it forms a seat or a backrest. Hooking on has become a habit.

The galley tap must meet three criteria. It must deliver water at a quantity to wash things properly and quickly, but not so much that your precious stock is wasted. It must work without committing one of your precious hands to pumping it. It

Julia strap-hanging in the galley.

shouldn't rely on electrics. I know electrically pumped water meets the first two criteria, but most blue water sailors have at least one story of a crew siphoning water through the tank breather in mid-ocean because the electric pumps had failed.

I once had a lovely brass pump with a long-lever arm, like those antique village pumps still seen in rural shires. It would have graced any Victorian gentleman's yacht. It was a proper pump, and replaced a cheap, nasty, squirty plastic job at the kitchen sink. The nasty squirty plastic job is now in use in *Petronella*'s heads, where it does just fine. The lovely brass long-lever-arm pump is back in its box somewhere, and I haven't seen it since it dawned on me that washing needs both hands but neither foot. I fitted a cheap, practical and unobtrusive foot pump which instantly made the galley more effective.

Preparation

- *A lot of preparation is needed. Remember all those heavily sponsored ocean racers who aren't ready in time.*
- *Be emotionally ready for the crisis. It will come. If you are lucky, you will derive some good from it. Good luck is more common than bad, otherwise our species would not have survived.*
- *Involve friends and crew. It's team work, all the way. Apologise to them later.*
- *Have a professional survey. Do everything it tells you to.*
- *Try all the vital new things before you go.*

How do I phone the Samaritans?

It is truly amazing how much has to be done to an already well-found boat to turn her into a safe ocean-crosser and home. I used to wonder why boats in ocean races and round-the-world events were never ready on time. Surely the corporate sponsors had put the start date in the skipper's Filofaxes? Why were they still fitting bits of electronics that they could have attached a year ago? Why were tins of baked beans still piled on the dockside the week before departure? Surely *Petronella* just needed to have her sweet bilges dusted and her decks painted reflective white to save our tender feet from the tropical sun – that and a few equally simple tasks. But the list grew longer even as I worked flat out. Everything took longer than estimated. I ferried car-loads of gear from London on every trip to her winter quarters in Cornwall, and now knew every chandler, sailmaker, rigger, steel fabricator and assorted marine and engine trade of Plymouth. Fire extinguishers, screws and fastenings, timber, electronics, liferaft, charts, pilot books, gas and plumbing and food cash-and-carry are just the tip of the supply iceberg that I got to know in Plymouth.

All boats are continuing works of art. Since buying *Petronella* in the spring of 1985, I have poured endless hours into making her fit for long-distance, short- and singlehanded sailing. She is happiest when I take her shopping. She is on her fourth self-steering system, if we count the short-lived attempt to sail her with an electronic autohelm. She began with no electronic navigation and has graduated to GPS via Decca. She has lost her 16hp, single-cylinder air-cooled Ducati diesel engine for a second-hand, 20hp, two-cylinder Bukh. The original wooden boom was so heavy and uncontrollable that I feared for my life when running by the lee. I made a new one from aluminium. The lifelines, stanchions, guard rails and trip-you-up-on-a-dark-night deck fittings have been redesigned and replaced. This is only a fraction of what has happened to her since meeting me. All in all, the *Petronella* sitting in a muddy Cornish creek all innocent of my Caribbean plans had better comfort, handling and equipment, and was much more ready for the ocean, than the *Petronella* I had taken across the Thames estuary towards the Azores in the summer of 1985.

Here are two sad facts you must live with. Not all seasons of an English year are equally suited to working on a boat. Not all months prior to a deadline command the same sense of purpose, commitment and urgency. Plan your work accordingly.

I have noticed that sailors dislike the cold and wet. Go into a boatyard over the winter and watch the people who live aboard or, worse, are sleeping on board at weekends to get more done, ha ha. They move at snail pace, with all the purpose of a hibernating bear. Like them, I did nothing in the deep mid-winter. Even when spring appeared and the weather improved, the best I could manage was half-hearted. Yet, thanks to friends, I had no lack of physical comfort to justify this tardiness.

Petronella had over-wintered in Cornwall, where two good friends of

Magnus learning some rope tricks.

mine, Mat and Fiona, live. When I began working on her seriously, I had their spare room to sleep in, kitchen to feed me, and a barn full of marvellous tools. This was an ideal location to prepare the boat and a perfect jumping-off spot for Spain, but I was living 250 miles away in London and working hard to stop work-ing. Something had to give as spring slipped into summer, and time pressed towards my sailing date. With so much gear to fit and jobs that needed the boat to be accessible and upright more often than the tide allowed, she had to come ashore. In late June, *Petronella* came out at a boatyard in Plymouth. Now I started work in earnest.

I had reckoned on being out of the water for two weeks. My two crew, Magnus and Julia, were standing by to work on the boat before we sailed in late July. I reck-oned without Fate. You will be hit by at least one crisis in your preparations. Try to get it in early. Try not to let it escalate into a catastrophe.

Oh goody, a crisis

As *Petronella* was being shored up in the yard I saw that her huge, 9 foot, barn door rudder was cracked along the waterline. My immediate joy at having such a last-minute reason to cancel my stupid trip was overturned by the assumptions of my

Cornish friends that I should shut up and start making a new rudder. Before I knew it, I was ordering plywood and epoxy.

I took the stoic stance that at least one potentially terminal crisis hits everyone, and that if I handled this one right, then Fate would save me from others. So I redesigned the rudder to build out the weakness where the break had occurred. Of course, the road to the next disaster was paved with over-specification. Modern marine ply is metric, not Imperial, and the sheets were thicker than before. This meant that the old galvanised gudgeons and pintles connecting the rudder to the hull were now too small. Making new ones, and various disasters in galvanising them and their nuts and bolts, took longer than the time I had spent making the new rudder. I suppose I should be grateful that the crisis on something so vital to the boat was still something I could tackle myself. And I suppose that I should be glad that I found a good marine engineering shop in Plymouth for the rudder steel work, because when I had to saw the stainless steel prop shaft in half as part of the Byzantine process to replace the propeller, I knew just the workshop to solve my problems.

Take heart. Before this, I had never made a rudder in my life or even dreamt of cutting a 1 inch stainless steel prop shaft with a hacksaw, never mind in such confined conditions. I managed it when I had to. Luck and chance rule this adventure of an ocean crossing, and I suppose in a Darwinian sort of way good luck is more common in life than bad.

The best of friends

An adventure like this is all team effort. Your friends will bear the brunt of your preparations and it is best to recognise this from the outset and draw them in with whatever charm and diplomacy you can muster. Mat and Fiona weren't the only friends I leant on but they provided tools, workshop, transport, accommodation, recreation, good company and much more. For example, they turned their kitchen over to us for almost a week while Magnus and Julia weighed and repacked food into plastic heat-sealed bags. Before and after, as well as in between, Magnus and Julia were painting and building on the boat, stowing and restowing and generally learning how things worked.

Friends can be judged by how much they will let you take advantage of them. In those last weeks before leaving Plymouth, I turned the life of Mat and Fiona upside down and took liberties with them that still make me blush. They never let me down for a moment. If you don't have friends like that, go out right now and get some.

One minute to midnight

The clocks change as your departure date gets nearer. You will not believe how much remains to be done in the last few weeks, and how rapidly a day goes by. With so much left to do I was spending hours just travelling. I had friends and family around the country to see. I had work to complete in London. At the last minute I sold my car and motorbike. I would have rented out my flat, but this was one hurdle too many.

The last-minute things we needed were coming from all over. I carted great piles of equipment around the country, including a new dinghy (which I could carry) and a liferaft (which I almost could not). I had too many things to take care of. No wonder the cans of baked beans of the ocean racing yachts take so long to get stowed.

I wouldn't have bothered with the last-minute boat survey if it hadn't been required by the insurers. It was worth doing. I knew *Petronella* intimately by now, but the surveyor told me three types of things, for which I am grateful: things that were fine and needed no further worry; things I didn't know needed to be improved; and things I knew about but was ignoring. He gave me a list, and the crew and I set to work. We did all the jobs he listed, except one. The lesson I learnt is: do them all. The surveyor said I should fit seacocks to all through-hull fittings. I went out and bought seacocks. It's just that I never fitted them. That one undone job nearly caused the loss of the boat in mid-ocean months later. We were lucky, but it caused a lot of fear when I was fighting off an African bug and really didn't need the extra exercise.

> **Log entry: day 3**
> The hull fitting for the bilge pump is leaking. The solution is obvious. Pull the brass junction out of the plastic pipe, clean it, smear it in lubricating detergent, warm the plastic pipe so that it becomes pliable, and then whack the whole lot together. Absolutely impossible in these conditions. I tighten the jubilee clips . . . this slows but does not stop the leak . . . I crawl out of the engine room and lie exhausted on the galley floor . . .
>
> I am worried. This is no time to be sinking. We are a few hundred miles off Africa with a whole ocean to drift across in a liferaft.

There are other reasons for a survey. It can help you through the totally unexpected things that may happen later. You may wish to sell the boat en route, renew insurance, prove seaworthiness or ownership. For more reasons that I can imagine, but will have happened to someone, you may be in a strange place, in need of a survey, without the time or local knowledge to get one.

I was trying to get all the really important jobs finished before we left England. This is not necessarily the right thing to do. There is a balance to be struck between how you spend your diminishing time and the cost to pay if that balance is wrong. I thought that the order of importance was the most sensible way to timetable jobs. With hindsight, I would have chosen the 'reverse order of universality', if you see what I mean. That is, I would have left till last the jobs I could just as easily do anywhere in the world, and do first those that I knew could only be done with the services and resources I could find at home.

Doing the jobs on your list is, of course, only part of the work they entail. When planning each job on the boat, think about where and when you will want to test this to see that it works. And then think about what you will need to fix it if it doesn't.

Passage planning

- *Build your plan around the big issues of weather and route. Nature has arranged the weather to help you make this journey.*
- *Collect the materials to detail the later stages of your journey, but don't bother reading them till you are on your way.*
- *Events and other people will change your plans, usually for the better.*
- *Flexibility is an attitude of mind that will come to you. Meet it halfway.*
- *A few events, such as finding the crew, fix your commitment to the adventure.*
- *Do some sailing too. Preparation isn't all about work.*
- *Home is not the only place where shops are. Fitting out can be done on the way, and some things more easily, but vital new gear should be tried before you leave. Sometimes even wood-screws are hard to find.*
- *It's better to be able to fix a broken engine than make it worse.*
- *You will never be ready. When it's time, just go.*

Shall we just go now?

We left England in hurry, even by my standards. The list of unfinished jobs on Petronella was not getting any shorter, and I still had things to do ashore, but a line had to be drawn somewhere – so I drew it and we sailed. This is very much the way of the whole trip. An opportunity or chance decision or some sudden pressure and off we go in response to it.

One defining moment in this adventure was signing my crew, Magnus and Julia. After that, my preparations for the crossing became very serious indeed and soon dominated my non-working life. These preparations had, of course, started long before then, and I would be misleading you to suggest that a first-time ocean crossing could be so lightly undertaken.

Like a couple of million others in the mid-1980s, when Prime Minister Thatcher knew no alternative to making the UK economy 'slimmer and fitter', I unexpectedly found myself with more leisure time than usual. I bought *Petronella* and went sailing in unwitting preparation for my Atlantic adventure.

The main pressure to leave on our Atlantic crossing was the worsening weather in Biscay as summer faded into autumn. This will be the case for all yachts from northern Europe, whether they come out of Scandinavia or Germany, Holland, Luxembourg or Belgium, France or Britain. All yachts from these countries must face Biscay, whether they chose to sail bravely across it or sneak around the edge. Surely few people want to face the weather in Biscay in November and December unless they are being paid to test thermal underwear? The likelihood of being caught by waves of 12 feet or over is slight in August, but a scary certainty in October.

Since we had already missed our planned departure date of July, I announced that August was the best time for a late crossing. September, I said, was too late, so of course it was September when we left Falmouth and my prophecy soon proved right. We sailed straight into a hard south-westerly that exhausted us before we were south of Ushant and into Biscay. Then we had the hardship of two gales and a 'hurricane' before tying up in Spain. I might have waited for a really good forecast and made Spain in five days instead of the eight it took us, but by the time we were ready to go, we were in a hurry just to get started.

I do not regret our timing of Biscay. I think it is courting disaster to knowingly put out into a gale, but there is something very reassuring about coming through bad weather unscathed. That, if nothing else we had done, made me feel we were ready for the Atlantic. We blew out the genoa, but so what? That was my fault, not the boat's. On an undertaking like ours, when sea crossings stretch outside the accurate period of a detailed weather forecast and the whole point is self-reliance and survivability, gales at sea just have to be written into the script. In my case, too, to do anything else would have involved a major character change and a lot more understanding of meteorology than I'll ever bring myself to acquire.

The main point about our leaving is why we left in a hurry in the first place. This is, after all, a lengthy undertaking. I had been partially planning this trip for ten years, had committed myself nine months earlier, and worked solidly on the boat through the whole summer. We wouldn't cross for another three or four months and the return was not till five months after that. A day or two on, the start barely mattered. So how did that hurried leaving come about? It's obvious. No boat is ever ready for a long sea passage. Life conspires against it. If you really want to go you just have to push off, mind full of doubts and a two-page list of jobs still pending.

Log entry: Biscay crossing
Magnus was looking intently at a sheet of white paper. I blushed. I hadn't been hiding it exactly, but nor had I been waving it about for the crew to read. It was headed 'Jobs for 1992'. That very long list had been prepared at least three years ago. Now I wasn't the only one on board to know the vintage of our undone jobs.

Our departure date was not set by me but by an equipment-hire company. It was the earliest date when the hired liferaft would be ready. I have never had a liferaft before, but I am older and wiser now and more cautious too. I collected the raft and bought some more safety harnesses, cursing that I had at last been caught out by my nonchalant attitude to harnesses. For years now I had carried four on the boat and had used them, at most, half a dozen times, but now I could not find them where I swore I had left them. To sail without them weighed as heavy as a superstition. Of course, there would be no disaster whereby we would need those harnesses, not unless we left without them. I also bought survival suits and wrote a list of safety gear to be packed in an emergency 'grab-bag', ready to come with us if we had to take to the liferaft. That is what I call being prepared.

In reality, we went through two Biscay gales with me feeling too unwell to search out the harnesses. The survival suits, whose purchase had so reassured me at the time, would not have helped much either, being stuffed right at the back of a clothes lock-er. The grab-bag, whose contents I had enthusiastically listed on paper, was stuffed so far back in my mind during those gales that it never occurred to me to fill one. And the essential liferaft that had determined our departure date was buried under two sails and some very wet and smelly oilskins. After the second gale had died down I fixed deck lifelines so that there was something to clip onto, but after the 'hurricane', the third and worst of our storms, I deliberately took off my harness when I went forward to raise the staysail. The sail change was difficult enough in a lively force 9 without a harness to confuse me. I told myself that we would organise this safety gear before we started our Atlantic crossing, even if by then the worst weather was probably behind us. We had the gear. It was just a matter of not yet having adjusted to having it. The getting of it was vital to our preparation. The using of it was not.

Beware in case you focus too much on matters of ultimate survival.[1] We failed to see the potential dangers in something much simpler. Our gas cooker. We didn't give enough thought to its unusually weak flame. We were probably half-poisoned

---

[1] Ultimate survival is a big topic. A point to consider is what a boat needs if it founders in reasonable weather, and what it needs if it is in some really awful storm. The Fastnet Race disaster of 1979 and the 'weather bomb' hurricane disaster north of New Zealand in 1994 both exposed the danger of relying on a liferaft in seas that are fierce enough to destroy competent ocean-going yachts. The real life-saver in the New Zealand storm was the EPIRB, an emergency device that signals to passing aircraft or satellites, and VHF radio.

Storm seas rising in Biscay; the waves took a long time to build into a proper Atlantic swell but by the first morning the confused surface waves had gone . . .

in Biscay by unburnt gas. A repair that would have taken two hours back in England amused us for a whole week at sea and in Spain, taking the cooker apart twice, rivets and olives included.

Plan in some fun

A sailing trip is about sailing even if most of your time is spent living, cooking, washing, cleaning and sleeping. Do not ignore the sailing in those last few over-full weeks before you leave.

When Magnus and Julia first arrived in Plymouth, Petronella was ashore and they had work to do. Then came launch day and we went for a sail. It did not matter that paint tins were crammed into lockers and tools shoved where they would rattle least. It was enough that we could slip out of the yard, hoist sail, and trip around the bay before coming into our new marina berth. It was wonderful, and every day after that I made a point of sailing, regardless of weather or work. Each afternoon had at least one hour set aside for sailing.

Some important steps can only be taken when the boat is on the water, and often only happen by chance. The blooding of Magnus was one of these. After launching I went back to London for a few days, leaving the crew on board. I asked Magnus to go sailing with Julia, hoping he would, but only half-convinced that he might. I came back to find that my crew and a visiting friend had sailed as far as the Plymouth breakwater. The extra muscle of the friend had given Magnus the confidence to take this big step. All had gone wonderfully well and even the docking

. . . and we had 15 footers rolling down on us.

29

had been done to perfection. Magnus stepped ashore a new man, only to find that his cowardly crew had never suspected he had the nerve to do the trip and had been in fear of their lives the whole time. Their new-found respect for him, now that their lives were not in danger, gave Magnus a greater appreciation of what he had achieved and a further boost in confidence. It was this, more than all our time at sea by then, that gave him the confidence to sail with Julia from Madeira to Porto Santo without me when I again had to leave Petronella to the pair of them.

A good read

The only vital passage planning before you set off is to get clear in your head the big picture of the weather, winds and currents of the Atlantic. These have been designed by Nature to help sailors from northern Europe escape their winter, so let the seasons determine your route. The detail can be filled in on the way.

After Biscay you slowly work your way south, keeping ahead of the northern winter as it too follows the sun. The prevailing westerlies that troubled you from Britain down to Biscay give way to northerlies once you pass Cape Finisterre. Now you have swapped head winds for the beam winds and following winds that will stay with you for the rest of your journey. Some time during November and December, anywhere from Madeira to West Africa, you will turn left to bring the winds of the trade belt astern. The magic carpet of current under your keel moves you westwards at half a knot.

When wind and current are going your way, navigation is surprisingly easy. Unlike sailing in Europe, the starting As and finishing Bs are now all in the right order. I have cried in frustration at adverse winds and tides when crossing the North Sea. My brain has turned to Spam trying to work out the best route across the Thames estuary, with its sandbanks and channels. I have sailed 70 miles off the coast of Brittany to avoid the tidal horrors of the Raz du Seine. It isn't that the conditions around Europe and Britain are always against you. The thing is: they are not always with you, and the moment comes halfway to anywhere when you feel you might as well turn back to where you started.

There is no rush. Even if you are late crossing Biscay, you have at least two months to sail the 2,000 or so miles to your preferred jumping-off point, and the places on the way deserve your time. Two things determine the timing and location of your departure point. First, to avoid the hurricanes that might still be coming out of the Caribbean even in November. Second, to hitch a ride on the trade winds as they move north and grow more reliable after November. Most yachts leave from the Canaries and drop south till they meet the trades. We didn't. We went farther south and left from Senegal.

All sorts of reference material exists to help you get the hang of this big picture, from the wonderful Admiralty plotting charts to the articles that routinely appear in the yachting magazines. Half a dozen or so standard books will give you an overview of Atlantic or world sailing routes. They usually have words like 'Atlantic' and 'sailing' and 'guide' in their titles. I bought two because I'm a nervous chap and

Ghosting along in the calm after the Biscay storm.

inclined to think that not reading two books makes for better preparation than not reading one. I also had World Cruising Routes because it's the sort of book a tea clipper skipper might have on his shelf, and I like other people to think I'm seriously into this business.

My most helpful advice from using these reference books is to make sure that at least one of them has good coloured pictures of national flags. Then get a couple of metres of sailcloth and some cloth paints. After this, wherever your lousy navigation or reckless disregard for planning leads you, you will always have the right courtesy flag. The cost of ready-made flags from a shop will feed the crew for a whole week or keep them in drink for half an evening, so avoid such waste if you can. By Sod's Law you won't go to all the countries you planned to and you will go to some you've never heard of. As you enter a new harbour under the searching eyes of officialdom, you will find in your locker every courtesy flag you bought except the one you need. Stay true to the vagabond spirit of ocean cruising and make your own flags. They will look awful on the cabin table when the paint is drying, but good enough when flapping at the crosstrees 20 feet up.

After the big picture comes the details of routes, landfalls and times. The heart of your cruising library is the local pilot books and the charts. Don't waste much time reading these before you set off. More important tasks should fill your life. Read these books only well enough to know which to buy, then buy the ones for all the areas you expect to visit. Spend a day or two in a good library, such as that of the Cruising Association, or browsing the shelves of a good marine bookshop. Choose carefully – pilot books and charts cost a lot of money, and Sod's Law applies here as much as to courtesy flags.

I was so anxious about buying pilot books and charts for faraway places that I nearly delayed leaving England. Don't. Most boats out there have the reference material you lack. Borrow or swap. Make sure you know your books well enough to know that they tell you how to make the landfalls ahead of you, then wrap them away in a nice dry locker. They are not interesting enough for bedtime reading. Turn to them when you need to flesh out the next passage and, later, when land hoves into sight.

More useful just now are the bite-sized chunks served up in the yachting press. These are written for entertainment, so you should be able to get from start to finish in the time it takes to let the filler harden or compose a tear-jerking letter to the taxman. Don't give up just because an article wants to tell you about every tack from Plymouth to La Coruña. There will always be some information in them for you. The time they were in the area. The good and bad weather. What little things failed or worked. What to have in your medicine cabinet if you are as accident prone as they were.

As we travelled south we came into increasing contact with more experienced long-term cruising boats. What was interesting was not just hearing their different plans, but seeing how these affected others. For example, the day we anchored in Madeira was the first time we heard about the wild adventures of cruising the West African coast. We were still too taken up with our own frighteningly adventurous plans of going straight to the Caribbean to do more than show polite interest, but a few days later we had a casual conversation with people planning to stop at the Salvagen Islands as they went down to the Canaries and this made us wonder about adding stops to our itinerary. A few weeks later we joined in serious conversations about the relative merits of the Canaries, Cape Verde Islands, Senegal, Gambia and Guinea Bissau. The plans we had made from comfortable armchairs during the previous winter were now so much a part of us that they had become a walk-through, no longer an adventure. We were shifting tack, becoming excited about the spiciness of a visit to Dakar and the West African rivers, and being comforted by the way other cruisers, much more experienced than us, were gripping these ideas.

Modification will happen to your plans, too. The only question is when and where. It only really happened to us after we had reached Madeira, because then we caught up with our year's pack of ocean-crossers. Had we had left England in

July instead of September, we might have come under their influence in Spain.

Our attitudes were becoming more flexible in ways that could not have happened while we were in England. People of our land lives wanted to hear how well organised and prepared we were. A detailed timetable and careful listing of itineraries became wonderfully reassuring, even saving long debates intended to test my sanity. But the mind-set of sea rovers is the reverse. The longer they have been blue water sailing, the more they seem open to major shifts of plan. This isn't because they are a link short of a chain, but because their life is geared to visiting new places. Don't hang on to your old mind-set too stubbornly.

They probably sell screws in Spain

When we arrived in Spain and the Atlantic islands, the great truth dawned that we could have left England earlier if we had planned some of our fitting-out as we went. Many of the things we needed were cheaper there, with better weather for painting and the like.

Start thinking like an ocean sailor before you become one. A sailing boat on the move has the potential to fit out wherever the supplies and conditions best suit. Don't think of home as where the shops are. Prior research might help if you have a specialist job in mind. Or even if you don't. We, for example, found that good paint was available in Spain and Madeira, but the yachty antifouling we applied in the UK was not. The solution: don't use expensive yachty antifouling. Use the local fishing brand.

Fishing boat chandleries in Spain are wonderful. Aladdin's caves of gear not found in England. Such wonderful galvanised fittings. I spend hours wondering how I might use this gear. I want to stock up since I may never see the likes of it again. I resist the temptation to buy Stockholm tar from a large barrel. Even I know I have no use for it.

We spent more time in ironmongers or *fereteria* than most English tourists in Spain, and what little Spanish I learnt is biased towards screws, paints, brushes and thinners. I also know the various precise meanings of words that a casual visitor might think translate into 'paraffin'. Most of them do not. I also learnt that the Spanish are ahead of the rest of Europe in giving up the use of paraffin lamps. I don't know what they use instead, but to admit that you still need a paraffin lamp is to knock your social status down a rank or three.

By chance, I also learnt about Julia. Her Spanish was better than Magnus's, so we left him to do ship-board tasks while Julia and I went shopping. We both benefited. I learnt a little of what made her tick. She learnt masses about fitting out a boat.

It isn't always possible to know what jobs can be done away from home. I deliberately gambled on doing one simple task on our way, and lost. As a result, the most vital of our special trade wind gear was not tried or tested until we were on passage from the Canaries to Africa, that last journey before the ocean crossing itself.

We left our mark in Porto Santo.

The classic trade wind rig is the twin foresails, where relatively small sails are poled out on either side. Most yachts that do a bit of racing, or usually sail with crew, will simply double up their spinnaker gear and run their poles and lines out on both sides of the boat. They will need new sails, but otherwise they are making only a minor modification to a familiar method. *Petronella* doesn't have spinnaker gear. Our solution was to tie a preventer[1] to the staysail to make it into one of the twin foresails, and pole out the jib for the other. All we had to do to mount the jib pole was screw sail-track on the front of the mast, fit a swivelling gooseneck to connect the track to the pole, and then mount sheaves onto the mast to take the three control lines needed to haul the pole up, down and out.

We had the bits, but we just didn't have time to fit the track before we left England. This hardly mattered since we had little chance of a following wind across Biscay. We could work out where the gear and lines should go as we wafted south, and all would be installed by the time we met the trade winds. Even now, writing this, it seems a perfectly sensible plan. I would still not have seen the flaw in it if I hadn't lived through the experience.

What was missing from our collection of gear when we left England were the wood-screws. Surely screws are available in Spain? How else do they hold their bull-rings together? But I wanted special wood-screws: short, fat, stainless steel, with large countersunk heads. They had to be short so they did not pierce the inch-

---

[1] A preventer is essential in downwind sailing. When a boat with sails right out rolls or the wind shifts slightly, the wind can get round from the back of the sail to the front. Then it lifts the sail and hurls it to the other side of the boat in a gybe. A line from the boom to a forward strong point prevents the sail from accidentally gybing.

thick walls of the hollow wooden mast. I did not want to put a screw through an electric wire. They had to be fat to get a good grip in such a short length. They needed large heads because of the size of the holes in the stainless steel track. They had to be countersunk to allow the traveller to slide up and down. I wanted stainless to avoid rusting or galvanic action. Here, I said to the crew as we landed in yet another Spanish harbour, pop off and buy us a dozen of these in the *fereteria*. I might as well have asked for thermal underwear in the Sahara.

Spain is a country of wonderful and frequent *fereteria*. We came down the Atlantic coast of Spain and never missed a single one, but not one of them had our screws. We left Spain with the track still in its locker. We loved the new *fereteria* of Madeira. So many. So colourful. But so lacking in wood-screws of the specified type. I travelled back to England for other reasons and returned with the wrong wood-screws. I misjudged the countersunk heads.

We sailed from Madeira to the Canaries with the track still in its locker and no proper way to pole out the jib. We loved the new *fereteria* of the Canaries. Just as many as Madeira. Just as colourful. But still no wood-screws. I carefully measured what was needed and phoned a friend who was coming out from London, giving detailed instructions. She arrived in the Canaries with the right ones. Now we had track up the mast. Now we had the lines fitted. Now, after goose-winging our way south almost to the coast of Africa, we at last had a pole to keep the jib out, but we would be in Senegal before we knew if it worked or not. This was cutting it a bit too fine – not to try our trade wind rig until we're down on the line.

Guardian angels don't fix diesels

Sailing boats need engines. I had already replaced Petronella's engine, to get rid of a very noisy air-cooled brute. I like the simplicity of air-cooled engines, but I needed a quieter, slightly more powerful engine to make my little yacht into a proper passage maker. I mean, I am more of a sailing purist than many, but when the choice is to motor for two hours to reach harbour or spend another night at sea, there is no contest.

We were sailing across the North Sea to Sweden. The wind died while I slept. The crew began to motor. I dreamed of being in a library with clanking robots. The more books I wanted, the noisier these metal librarians clanked. Bits were falling off them. I had a report to finish and couldn't concentrate. The more I shushed at them, the louder they clanked. I woke sweating, with a pounding headache. It took one minute to realise the cause of my nightmare. That engine had to go.

Even little modern diesel engines need to be maintained and, since at times you will be totally reliant on your engine, you should have an elementary understanding of its workings and a good stock of spare parts. Don't be put off buying things like a spare injector or water pump by the criminally high prices. It cost me a lot to have a small bag of parts sent out to the Canaries.

One lesson I learnt the hard way, and will no doubt learn again, is that diagnostics is the key to fixing faults. I have a tendency to get the diagnosis wrong. Given a choice of two, I will pick the wrong one. I wish my guardian angel would take a proper course in marine diesel engines. I think mine studied military strategy. My guardian angel is always ready to fix the previous fault, but not the current one.

Coming in to one of the Spanish rías the wind dropped and we decided to motor the few miles to harbour. We had no sooner tied the sails neatly for the night when the engine stopped. It stopped with that thump when a line has wound incompressibly tight round the prop shaft. We hung over the stern but saw no trailing ropes, so it had to be air in the fuel line. This made sense. We had periodically been bleeding air since I had fitted new fuel lines in Plymouth.

I wanted to bleed the lines in harbour rather than while drifting in the dark, so we pressed the starter and the engine sprang into life. A few minutes later it stopped again. No rope around the prop and no obvious problem when I opened the engine compartment, so I fiddled a bit and tried the starter again.

When the engine thudded to a stop again we untied the sails and hoisted them. We half-sailed, half-drifted out of the ría until we were far enough offshore to lash everything down for the night. Julia took first watch, then me, then Magnus. It was nearly midnight by the time we turned in. Magnus and I cursed the rolling as we flopped around in our berths or got up to stop the cups or plates or whatever was murdering our sleep. An hour later I relinquished sleep and got up to fix the engine.

Over the next four hours I bled the fuel system with increasing facility and in a variety of ways. I worked in one of two positions. I either half-draped myself over the flywheel to avoid crawling into the engine compartment, or I crawled in and crouched bent double by the side of the engine. And all the time the boat was trying to roll its decks under.

I was resting in the cockpit admiring the distant land with its promise of a stationary bed when I realised I was trying to solve the wrong problem. I suddenly had the hot flush of stupidity and a glimpse into the void of my mechanical ineptitude. There was, after all, a third explanation for the refusal to run and I did not like it.

During the night I had been running the engine at intervals to see if fuel was getting through. To begin with the engine only stopped turning when I banged over the decompression lever. Later it would not even turn while decompressed. This was clearly not due to air in the fuel. I thought it was due to a flattened battery, so I recharged with our emergency generator. The fully charged battery produced a really solid 'dumph!' as the pistons moved a fraction of an inch before stopping dead in the cylinders. My tired brain sensed that this had nothing to do with air locks or battery state, and everything to do with piston lubrication. Or total lack of it. I sat in the cockpit in a sweaty flush of panic wondering whether my persistence had by now caused the engine to seize. Did I have an engine or a new reserve anchor?

I climbed down to the engine compartment and pulled out the oil dipstick. Nothing. I wiped it, put it back, and looked again. Still nothing. Eureka!

I was glad that Julia and Magnus were asleep. I did not have to explain my incompetence until I could put a gloss on it. I got out the engine oil. I trickled some into the rocker cover and gently cranked the pistons back and forth on the starter handle, repeating this until the pistons moved smoothly. Then I filled up with oil, gave the decompressed engine a few short bursts on the starter motor, until it was time for the real thing. I whacked over the decompressor and let the engine fire. I ran it for ten minutes with my head over the stern watching the exhaust smoke. It was bluer than I remembered, but not as awful as it might have been. I engaged gear and ran us offshore for half an hour. We had an engine that worked, even if we might have lost a few of the 20 horses we nominally called on from Mr Bukh.

We were lucky and I learnt a third tactic in the eternal battle of mechanical engineering. I do not suppose that being able to think of three reasons why the engine won't work would get me a diploma, but it is one more reason than I could think of that day.

In the late morning Julia and I were raising sail when a 50 foot, blue water rust-stain flying the French flag motored up. The villainous-looking skipper turned off the engine and the whole world went quiet again. We spoke as best we could in our different languages and the skipper commented that there was not enough wind to sail. I could not even begin to find the French to describe the vulnerable state of our engine and my reluctance to use it until we were within spitting distance of harbour. 'We always sail,' I shouted, 'even if it means an extra day.' The man looked suitably impressed as he fired up his unsilenced engine and scrunched it into gear. It blew out genuinely worrying oil-black smoke as he opened the throttle and went on his way like a tractor. Do I really have anything to worry about with this engine?

Crew

- *Of all the things you must get right, this one matters most. Think about it. Work at it. If you aren't all having fun, fix it.*
- *Requirements for crew are physical and social: physically adventurous, good balance, strong constitution, communicative and able to deal with authority.*
- *Try to get a mix of personalities and social skills, for life ashore as well as on board.*
- *It's living on a small boat that causes the problems. Cramped space and endless motion wreak havoc with the best-balanced psyches. Watch for this. Have a plan.*
- *I blame the skipper. Skippers have the final responsibility for a good crew, but must involve all the crew in solving problems.*
- *Voyages have beginnings, middles and ends, and each stage brings different stresses to life on board. Look for the patterns.*
- *Equality works best. This isn't Nelson's Navy.*

There's nowt so queer as folk

Making a good crew matters above most other things because crossing the ocean must be fun if it is to have any point at all. Making crew good is a long business, but it helps to have the right individuals to begin with. And that means having the right skipper too. When I say 'crew' I really mean the whole bunch of comrades on board, regardless of status and function. The only reason I might stress the viewpoint of the skipper is that this is where most of the choosing of others and action to shape them originates.

We can all work on our strengths and weaknesses. The trick is to know which is which and which way lies improvement. Before this adventure began I had already dabbled at all the things a sailing skipper does, and that included managing crew. I was not even bad at being a skipper in those days – sometimes. This trip deepened my knowledge of every aspect of sailing, but it taught me most about how people meld as crew. I had thought hard about how we would all get on and what my job would be in this. I thought, I read, I chatted. I was well prepared, as far as preparation means anything. Doing it is different. This trip showed me that good crew management need not be difficult, but it usually is. I want to help change that.

Our experiences revealed some factors affecting crew relations, which most writers don't dig into very deeply. From these I hope to derive conclusions to ease your sailing life. Of course, in crewing, like much else about this trip, events happen with their usual randomness and then you live with what follows.

Skippers tend to live too much in their own world, with their own worries and problems. The sailing literature is littered with skippers who score F double-minus in human awareness. There they all are, banging on elegantly about the trials of living with a spineless crew on the verge of revolt, with never a thought for how they have brought normal, sturdy individuals to this crisis. Bad practice. Unfortunately, what most of us learn from bad practice is how to do things badly.

It was the best of crews. It was the worst of crews. Sometimes we brought out the best in each other. Other times we seemed to be unravelling our egos. At times we were three murderers in close confinement, unable to leave our corner of the boat for fear of meeting the others. Kill or be killed, the motto of any crew after a week at sea.

The lessons all three of us learnt are among some of the most important lessons of this book. Not just because good relations make the journey enjoyable, but because good relations can never be taken for granted. If you have a good hull today, you will still have a good hull tomorrow. And the same for the rig. But there's nowt so queer as folk and what seemed like friendly banter over breakfast can come like a knife through armour at supper.

Here are two ways to judge whether a crew is good or not. First, the rulebook way of whether they can hand, reef and steer; second, the more self-indulgent way of whether they are team players and fun to be with. Remember that this isn't the sea cadets of some minor public school nor even the Royal Navy of Nelson's day. Don't put too much weight on practical sailing experience. Anyone will learn with

Julia soon got the hang of checking the wind direction.

time, and time is what you will certainly have. I doubt that the fighting skippers of Nelson's Navy ever thought to choose amusing conversation over the ability to make a quick eyesplice in 3-inch manila while boarding the enemy for a bit of mutual cutlassing. You should.

I had a good crew, from start to finish, so I have something for you to emulate. We started as a weak crew so far as sailing knowledge and boat handling went, but long before we cast off from Africa we were a crew that could sail our stubborn little boat anywhere. If we ended up barely on speaking terms that is still better than some other crews I have met, and there are lessons there for you too.

A crewed commitment

Finding crew might not have been the pivotal arrangement of this adventure, but it was the one that anchored the idea to a timetable. I might sail the boat across alone if I had to. *Maybe*. However, taking someone with me put out a social obligation stronger than any personal one.

The moment came almost by accident. It was Christmas. I was with friends when the conversation turned to my sailing plans. A plan had been taking shape in my sailing dreams for a month or more, but I had yet to talk about it. I gave a tentative preface about the challenge of crossing an ocean, and then I hit the no return button. I turned to Magnus, the eldest son of my friends, and said: 'I need crew, especially if I have to leave the boat to get back here when work demands. Do you want to come?'

Magnus

I never doubted that Magnus would be excellent crew. The previous summer he had been crew when I sailed to Spain. Between fixing himself a job in Madrid and entertaining his girlfriends, he had been my main crew that whole summer. We had brought the boat back across Biscay from La Coruña to Falmouth in a single shot.

Magnus has an easy way with people and we have got on well since we first went sailing. He has many qualities that will make him a good sailor, but he has two that are truly wonderful: a cast-iron stomach and a gift to read the landscape from the chart accurately. He shares both of these qualities with his father. I came to trust his pilotage and navigation more than my own.

He turned out to be better crew than I could have expected, and got better every day.

Magnus was home briefly from his job of teaching English in Madrid and in the mood to swap that work for something new. Now I had put him on a timetable that involved quitting work and coming back to England in July or August. That put me on a timetable to get myself and the boat ready by then.

And then we were three

Magnus and I agreed to get in touch at Easter. Apart from that commitment, I left the arrangements with him suitably vague. Even so, I knew I was now on my way to a crossing. This was confirmed around Easter when I had a call from Magnus to check when I wanted him in England. This had me scrabbling around for my list of outstanding jobs and a serious look through my diary at my work commitments. A week later I had a call to say that Magnus had the third crew member lined up and when did I want to meet her?

What third crew? I had completely forgotten that I had said we should get a third hand. I had done nothing about finding one myself. Indeed, I had drifted to the conclusion that since none of my regular sailing friends could spare the time, this adventure would just be Magnus and me. I figured out what extra food, water, safety gear and so on was implied by a third person, revised my list of jobs to be done, and a month later I met Julia.

Julia had done no sailing but was obviously an adventurous sort. She had left California a couple of years before, shortly after finishing college, to travel in Europe. She had gone to Madrid to work and learn Spanish, and had met Magnus there. She was ready to go home, and a slow boat across the ocean seemed like a good idea.

> **Julia**
> Julia was the great unknown. I spent a lot of time wondering if she was making out as one of the crew. Perhaps I had good reason to, but perhaps too much attention on something isn't healthy. Like pulling a plant out of the pot to see if its roots have taken.
>
> She made a good start in Cornwall and impressed me coming across Biscay. She was very brave in the gales and also later as the journey continued. She added to the good feeling on board. She had a strong constitution and good balance. She even managed to learn some navigation in Biscay, and navigation, being a head-down activity, is third only to cooking and mending the heads in inviting seasickness.

I had no idea how Julia would work out as our third crew member, but I trusted Magnus's judgement. One of the first questions I asked him was whether they were 'an item'. I'm not sure now why I thought I needed to know this, but it seemed important for a dozen reasons at the time. I'm egalitarian. I asked Julia as well. It seemed they were just good friends and that was fine by me.

We agreed that Biscay was the test to decide whether Julia could make the Atlantic crossing. In Spain I wanted all three of us to be happy that Julia should come, as a way of making all of us responsible for the trip and to feel equal ownership of the venture. That was probably why I wanted to know about any romantic attachment between my crew. I had no objections, but I did want to know whether it was Magnus's head, heart or hormones I was taking advice from. The bad weather in Biscay tested us and welded us as a crew. By the time we arrived in Spain, Julia was on the crew list.

Sweet music of the spheres

Having a mix of personalities and ages on board helped us to meet people every-where we went. The tensions that built up while we were caged together at sea evaporated very quickly when we were on land. They often built up again during our time at anchor, but that goes without saying. Harbours rot men and ships alike. These tensions evaporated the day we put to sea. That might be a bit of a gloss on the reality as we lived it, but so what? We deserve all the gloss we can get.

I imagine that the same cycles of tension and release apply to all crews, much as they do to good mouth-organ music.[1] We had our share. There must be a good chance with any crew that relations end with some supernova of a bang. The point, however, is this: I think we got more from the world out there, and more from what we encountered in that world, than most of the crews I have met.

On *Petronella* we each tended to do more of some tasks than others. Magnus was our main cook and I was third reserve. Both happened for good reasons. Cook is nearly as big a job as skipper. One person should not do both all the time. Magnus happens to have a gift with food and I happen to have the opposite. So Magnus was most often in the galley and never seen doing some of the other routine work, such as sail repair. Perhaps he thought Julia should have a steady job of her own, although it might have been because he was hopeless at sewing. Anyway, I only had to men-tion that we had another torn seam in the staysail, or arrive on the foredeck with the sewing kit, and Julia would be there. Magnus wouldn't even stir.

Julia's natural role on board was cabin-boy. The junior member, with most to learn. She made a pretty good shot at this. It can be tiring when it involves being the butt of the others' jokes. Any skipper should make sure this is not overdone. I think both Magnus and I were rather proud of our cabin-boy and I hope our jokes reflected this. She was the only one of us to go to the top of the mast to fix things, and she did it more than once. Anyway, Julia gave as good as she got and this, indeed, was one of her key roles. She could jerk Magnus out of his torpor when I couldn't, and remind him that we had work to do when he had skiving in mind.

Seagoing roles need not carry over into those we have on land, and nor should the skipper always lead the parade. Other sailors and officials seem to have more fixed ideas about this, and we managed to confuse a few of them, but I have good memories of the way we slipped in and out of roles to suit circumstances. This isn't to say that we changed character. Quite the opposite. We gained comfort because we seldom had to take roles that ran counter to our personal character. This was just luck. We gelled that way. It wasn't thought through in advance.

One role never changed. Magnus was always our social secretary and envoy to the

---

[1] I was trying to learn the mouth-organ on the trip. The lesson book went on a lot about cycles of tension and release. I have yet to master the instrument.

outside world. He loved being in all the places and circumstances where new people are met. Julia and I were much more reticent. We relied on Magnus to take the lead in a social event.

The relationship between skipper and crew also doesn't change much, but its character should. It seemed odd at times that we had more clearly marked and hierarchical roles when ashore than when at sea, but I think on the whole we benefited from it. Time ashore for the crew meant socialising and seeing the sights. For me it meant getting the boat ready for the next passage. There is never enough time for this. Any skipper will feel driven to keep working on the boat and want to see the crew busy too. But a driven crew is not a happy crew. The point of sailing is not to get blisters from perfecting the varnish.

I spent a lot of my time trying to balance our different needs while attempting to get the maximum amount of work done with the most fun. It often seemed to me that I took very tight control over our time, but I thought it vital never to show this. I dislike dictatorial skippers. I dislike crews that need a dictator. We saw too many of both. I got a real sense of satisfaction when people ashore could not tell whether Magnus or I was the skipper.

Things changed once we put to sea. Then it seemed natural that the requirements of the boat dictated what was to be done, and vital that we all develop the sea-senses to feel what these were. By the time we left Spain for the Atlantic islands we all had a sense of ship-board tasks. Most routine things just seemed to happen. There was less need for lists and timetables. But, of course, if anyone thought a list was needed, anyone could make one. Most of the time we just had to talk about what needed to be done for some group sense of action to emerge.

Magnus unruffled after the Biscay storm.

Falling out with Freud and Jung

A happy crew is a talking crew. I was pleased that we developed a number of conversational themes as we sailed. One was about sailing *Petronella* into the South Seas, which rather appealed to me as a prospect as well as a sign that we were happy together on the boat. Another was about the restaurant that Magnus and Julia would set up. This involved long lists of meals, and was probably just a variation on a theme that occupies most crews: their bellies and filling them.

An unheard-of event. Magnus complains of seasickness. We almost started to worry when the big lad lost his appetite two days later. We were not quite calling for a medical helicopter but we did change our main topic of conversation. Magnus shunned all talk about starting a beach restaurant on the other side of the ocean.

I liked it that our sailing topics were quite different from our harbour conversations. In harbour we were working on the boat or sightseeing, or meeting other people, and the talk was all about how to do things, how to get to places, and who these characters were around us. Our talk ashore included others. When sailing, our topics reflected the separate world we occupied, and the task we had to the exclusion of other people. The sea set the mood for our conversations. Slower than the land and more introspective. Long periods of time alone on watch build thoughts to try out on the others. Long periods wondering how the others are coping with our life. The easy relationships that come from knowing that we all share these conditions. Signs of problems on board usually came when the conversation stopped.

Darkening skies

The skipper has the main duty of seeing that the crew is getting along well. It is vital that they do. A crew that isn't having fun is not capable of the independence and sustained commitment to the common good that boat safety depends on. It was a very bad sign for me when, half-way to the Caribbean, I realised that I was losing sympathy with Julia who seemed to me to be withdrawing and gathering a little black cloud around her. I was resentful that she was making this offshore adventure of blue sky and frisky seas into a depressing experience. The line I took in trying to sort things out just made her withdraw more. The exchanges between us seemed to become more brutal.

Part of the problem, I suspect, was that Julia and I were similar in one vital respect. We both tended to internalise our problems and worries. Two people like that are not naturally going to sort out difficulties that impinge on one another. During the time on our crossing when I wanted to solve the problems of Julia's black cloud, rather than just cast it adrift to let it find any home so long as it wasn't near me, I had two ways of tackling it. First, my own amateur psychoanalysis of what was happening. Second, advice from Magnus. At least I had some clue about who on board was best able to deal with a couple of introverts like Julia and me.

Of course, my psychoanalysis was even less well informed than my other ventures into marine specialisms, such as weather forecasting, navigation and diesel engines. My subtlety was at its lowest when I asked Julia directly why she had ceased to function as a member of the crew. I'm afraid the words 'pain in the arse' may have been spoken. My good friends Freud and Jung would not have been impressed by my approach.

On reflection, I don't think that taking advice from Magnus was much help. Magnus was a conduit between Julia and me. I found it reassuring when he said he had no idea what I meant by her 'black cloud'. I assumed I was either too sensitive to these matters or was inventing something that wasn't there. It never occurred to me that Magnus was taking sides, other than my own of course. This may not have been a bad thing for him to do – for the sake of the boat I mean – since we got where we were going all in one piece. I rate Magnus's natural judgement highly, but this advice just made me put the problem to one side, where it festered. It might have been better to bring one set of problems, mine or Julia's, into the open: My cod-psychoanalysis; Julia's retreat into a shell.

A nagging question

Although Julia was on the crew list when we arrived in Spain, there remained a question mark over her for me. All boats with crew must run up against the question of whether someone should be put off or not. This is probably the most important decision any skipper on a first-time crossing will have to make. I can tell you two things. First, it isn't easy to take. Second, if you reach that awful decision point once, you will certainly find yourself there again.

For skipper or crew, the conventional trade wind route forms a series of staging posts giving opportunities for reassessment of the crew:

⬥ *From Biscay* Spain is the first chance to assess the crew, but you are so glad to arrive and there is so much to do on the boat that the decision is easily made. Onwards.

⬥ *To Madeira* An easy sea passage and the first real fun. So not a lot of pressure to put anyone off.

⬥ *At Madeira* Scope here for questions to be raised, but this isn't the best place to drop someone wanting to get back to the UK, so the tendency is to paper over the cracks.

⬥ *To the Canaries* Not a hard sail, so not much different from the trip to Madeira. If anything, sailing in the south lulls you into rose-tinted visions.

⬥ *At the Canaries* Tension in those exposed harbours, and pressure that this is the last place to prepare and provision the boat. It won't be easy to put crew off in Africa but even so the thin chance of it lets the final decision slip by.

⬥ *To Africa* All excitement now, so no one behaves badly and the question slips out of sight.

⬥ *In Africa* A mix of excitement and tensions at so many strange people and places. This is the last chance, isn't it? Oh well, I expect all these doubts are just the effect of land again, and everything will work out fine when we go sailing.

The decision at last started to weigh heavy in the Canaries. I knew I was delaying our departure when we were still there after three weeks, but it took ages to dawn on me that it was because I had not resolved whether Julia was coming or not. This single question had deep ramifications.

Cash-and-carry crisis

The final crisis in the Canaries came when we stocked up in the excellent cash-and-carry. There would be serious consequences if we got this provisioning wrong. I wanted as much as we could carry of these good foods at those cheap European prices. I guessed that things would be short in Africa and expensive in the Caribbean.

Provisioning was down to Magnus, with Julia helping, but in the cash-and-carry they wandered indecisively, discussing brands of tinned tomatoes and so on, but not actually loading cases onto the trolley. To speed things up I would go off to get things for the trolley, but when I came back there seemed to be less on it than before. Finally our drifting got us almost to the check-out, and then it became obvious that our kitty system had just collapsed. No cash. I was thankful that the problem had re-formed itself into a simple and practical one of getting money from a hole-in-the-wall rather than the more fundamental ones of whether we have all we need and why we have been messing around. Magnus and I ran off to sort this out. Perhaps I should have spent some time wondering whether we were failing on the most fundamental question of all for a crew: are we all pulling in the same direction?.

As usual, I asked Magnus what was wrong. There was a whole bag-load of bad things jumbled up here. There was the serious matter of whether the provisioning fiasco had left us short of the things we would need at sea. There was Magnus's responsibilities for provisioning, and whether I should undermine this. There was our relationship, and whether I was right to tackle the question of Julia through him. In the end I retreated into practicalities. I didn't challenge him on our provisions. Instead I went to a little supermarket and bought the things that seemed lightest to me. I accepted that there would be some shops in Africa if we found out in a couple of weeks' time that we had run out of something essential. I didn't challenge Magnus when he said Julia seemed fine. I let him speak to her, and took his word that she would pull her weight. There was still the chance for reassessment in Africa. As so often, we did what works best on a sailing boat. We all went sailing.

Of course we were all equals

At some point the relationship between skipper and crew runs up against the problem of authority. Your choice is where you draw the line. In my head I saw *Petronella* as a floating republic of egality. Of course, I have no idea if this idyllic vision of trio-dom was shared by the crew. I would have balloted them if I had thought they would deliver me my preferred answer.

On little offshore boats our attitudes towards authority still come from the ambient social values of the worlds we have just left and this was a key to much that happened between the three of us. We had quite separate attitudes, which came out of our different histories, and which were so deep-rooted that we could not change them to meet our new circumstances.

My inclination to let everyone help shape the working relationships on board seemed, from outward appearances, to work better for Magnus than for Julia. But then, he had the easier role of the two of them. He already knew me. He was the one I had invited. He knew we got on very well. He has the wit to use humour and goodwill to diffuse conflicts and is the most naturally Machiavellian of us all. He also had a junior under him, to boost his ego if that was ever needed. But, apart from that, Magnus is not the sort to be uncomfortable with authority.

> **Playing the skipper**
> A boat can only have one skipper, but it doesn't have to be Captain Bligh.[1] The skipper has to know when to stand on authority and when to let it slip.
> After about a week out from Africa the crew muttered about changing the main meal from evening to midday. I was reluctant to give way. I mentally huffed and puffed and preened my authority in case it was being undermined. In the end, I gave way. The crew had as much right as I to choose the main mealtime. I mean, should I be telling them how to dress for dinner as well? Hmmm, perhaps.

Julia had a very different attitude to authority, rooted in childhood experiences of family break-up. We talked enough about this when we came together at the beginning, but not enough for me to know how best to relate to it. Julia's childhood battles gave her traits that were enormously valuable to us on board, but perhaps she had a limited endurance of authority.

If you are taking crew on your trip, you need to understand their attitudes to you and yours to them. And since no one has all the skills and sensitivities to do this, get their contributions to help you out.

New routes to respect

The new technologies of seafaring also imply new relations on board. Prior to electronic navigation, a ship's captain lived with a high degree of ignorance in vital areas. I mean, goodness me, he didn't even know what time it was until Harrison invented the robust chronometer two centuries ago. Most critically, the captain didn't know with precision where the ship was and what course it should take to get to its planned destination. So, like all ignoramuses in positions of power, he had to protect his authority by social isolation and a flog-'em-and-hang-'em brevity of conversation. He practised the high arts of mystification common to all classes of disciplinarian. Baffle the poor souls before they realise it's all empty pretence. Deliver indisputable orders at military volume and at confusingly short intervals.

---

[7] I mean no disrespect to Captain Bligh. He was, after all, a very great navigator and motivator. A recent history of the Mutiny on the *Bounty* shows him as a relative liberal for his time and a victim of Fletcher Christian's libido. I merely pass this snippet on. I am no expert in these matters.

Log entry: towards Africa
A dark but starry night. The crew sleep their sleep of the innocent, and balmy winds drift over my fifth glass of Spanish cooking red. I have a revelation. It is that even in my inebriated state I can still calculate our position on the globe and the course to our destination with a precision undreamed-of by Captains Bligh and Cook, Britain's finest navigators, whose professional boots I am not fit to wipe. A second revelation follows fast. I am not the only person on board who can manage this miracle of navigation. The two snorers can do it just as well. What will keep my place in the pecking order?

Well, if this is the line you like to take yourself, I have bad news for you. The world of technology has pulled the rug out from under your feet. The most highly regarded information on a ship at sea is at everyone's fingertips. We are all democrats now.

With GPS my crew expect to know exactly where they are whenever they want. They expect to know the distance, direction and time of arrival at any point in the world that interests them, whether it is the place we last left or where we intend to arrive. They press a button and expect to have this information by the time they have cleaned their teeth or put the kettle on.

They are competent to direct the course of the boat on any passage, to make full sense of the charts and other arcane materials of the navigator, and to feel no reluctance in voicing an opinion during passage-planning. I can't assert superior knowledge when I no longer want to go to those wilder places we once agreed on. I have only the truth to tell in this world of equals and this, when stripped of the usual verbiage, just boils down to one sort of fear or another. So now the really valuable education I must give the crew is why so much of my sailing experience provides valid reasons for fear. And to do this in the hope that at least I can have a convincing reason for still being skipper. Well, that is as good a definition of democratically legitimated power as any in the textbooks of political theory.

The enemy within

Let's leave personalities aside for a moment. This isn't really about personalities. The point is that the relationship between crew and skipper is an interesting one, as Freud might have remarked to Captain Bligh, or Jung to Mr Christian. The skipper doesn't have to appear to the crew like a red rag to a bull, even if the converse is less obviously true. It helps if you can get a handle on what is degrading the normal goodwill between shipmates but this does not always enable you to solve the problem.

Beware of seizing on the obvious. Your vision of the problem won't be the same as the crew's. It won't even be as accurate as theirs. Your caring sensitive, in-depth assessment of crew relations, done in undisturbed isolation from the crew, will surely only make the glaringly obvious symptoms of misunderstanding even more glaring – like some trophy that you compulsively polish. The unwise skipper is then

Magnus had a laid-back attitude.

unshakable in his/her insistence on dealing with the symptoms rather than the cause and so adds yet one more cause to the real problems.

Friction and misunderstanding creep up on everyone on board because it is in the very air you breathe. Oh my, but it took forever for this penny to drop for me. I mean, there we all were, sardined into a little sailing boat that wouldn't keep still long enough for us to scratch in comfort. What effect did all that physical dislocation have on our emotional states? We stood watches every live-long day and never realised that when some of us were wide awake and raring for noise and action, others were bitchy with tiredness and wanting to be left alone. No wonder tensions seemed to grow as land grew nearer and then to dissolve as soon as our anchor dropped.

Seasickness is a factor

One constant part of our sailing lives was the continuous motion of the boat. I know seasickness takes many forms, but I don't think I fully appreciated this during our adventure. I don't think I realised that it would stop my brain from giving proper thought to the lesser events of our lives, such as just getting through each day.

Heading out towards Biscay I watched to see who would suffer from seasickness. After that I stopped observing. Magnus was immune to seasickness, Julia probably immune, and I wasn't. As a result of some doubtful logic, I concluded that when I wasn't feeling sick, no one else would be. I also believed what I told the others: that I was sick in the first two days and fine after that.

My analysis failed to recognise that seasickness is more subtle than a sweaty green complexion, serial vomiting and wishing for death to take us – now. Yet I know many sailors who get sick whenever the weather gets rough, even if they have been at sea for a week or more. I met a singlehander in Grenada who crossed from the Canaries in 31 days and vomited on most of them. I should have assumed that if others were caught out after they had their sea legs, then we would be too. I should have probed behind the highly visible forms of disorientation to ask myself what lesser symptoms to expect on *Petronella*, and when.

Part of the terrible insidiousness of the underlying causes of friction is that they work away at everyone's mental alertness. We were lucky on *Petronella* because we had a natural peacemaker in Magnus. But, of course, the conditions of our world conspired against us. It is just a matter of time before *no one* is in the right frame of mind to back off, and to recognise that something needs to be done. I think a little notice might help, written in 3-inch-high letters in luminous ink and stuck on every bulkhead of the boat, saying: 'Feeling murderous again? It isn't just you. Remember The Plan?' And then, of course, you need a Plan, otherwise your notice doesn't make sense. And this Plan is the most important thing we never had and you must make sure that you do.

Sometimes the ocean was just too much to take.

The Plan

The Plan is something you all discussed and agreed back in the Nag's Head or wherever, when the trip hadn't started and the goodwill was flowing freely. The Plan is what you intend to do when the inevitable effects of permanent motion and cramped living start to destroy you all. And the point is that you really have to sit down together and talk about this, so that you can recognise that it will happen and must be dealt with.

We train our bodies for the physical abuse they will take on this journey, and our hands and minds for the knowledge and instinctive dexterity they will need to sail the boat. I even read half a book on how to care for diesel engines and Magnus went on a one-day first aid course. That is how seriously well-trained we were. But how many of us read manuals on management or take a course in psychology before we ask a group of semi-strangers to go beyond anything they or you have experienced before? I did some deliberate team bonding at the outset, when it was easiest and I could still remember, but I should have done much more once we were under way. It needn't be big or contrived. We only needed one moment in every day when someone was praised or rewarded or asked to do something gratuitously indulgent, for no other purpose than to show that their contribution to our joint endeavour was appreciated. All crew members need this equally, whatever evil you entertain as their true just deserts.

Hypothesis, antithesis, synthesis. Eureka!

It makes a lot of sense to divide a sailing passage up into a beginning, a middle and an end, and the same applies to this adventure as a whole, even if its middle bit might be somewhat obscured. Different things are happening in our heads and bodies at these different stages. It should not be a surprise to anyone that these are then translated into funny relationships between companions on the journey.

Beginnings, middles and ends each have their own tensions. Moods shifted as each departure day arrived and shifted yet again once we were safely out to sea. I sensed these shifts but it never occurred to me to think harder, to see what things were common and recurring. You should become more aware than I was of how these aspects of the blue water life affect your social behaviour.

No corpses

This has been a fair run around the snags of living with a crew, but let us not get life-as-we-knew-it on *Petronella* out of perspective. All animals have fears, but human beings can create stress just by thinking. We can heighten worries into neuroses, and then medical researchers alone know what is happening within our bodies and our brains. A few minutes or even hours of stress is harmless, normal, what we are built for. Who knows, though, what effect comes from the days and weeks of stress we faced on our journey. So let's celebrate and rejoice in the good things. We came into harbour at Tobago, dropped anchor, and no one on board shot anyone else on board.

A few days after we had arrived in Tobago an official came to the harbour with a form for all skippers to complete. Did we have the same number of live crew now as when we left our last port and, if not, how had they died and been disposed of? How droll. This surely was a wind-jammer question, when galleons clogged up the horse latitudes for weeks on end and skippers decided the crew was worth less than the horses. The official and I laughed about how it didn't apply to modern yachts.

A tiny yacht from Spain had arrived in Tobago a few hours before us, after 32 days crossing from the Canaries. We met them in Kim's bar that first evening. The two-man crew were recovering their spirits rapidly. Their English was sluggish, but they communicated with everyone at the bar well enough. They held the bar chairs with white knuckles and gyrated wildly in a language-free impression of life on a

I'm not sure if a steel helmet was really necessary.

trade wind sea. The rum flowed, life was good again. Later we heard more of the darker side of their 32 days at sea. One of the crew had come close to suicide, depressed by the ineluctable rolling. The other would, I think, have willingly helped dispatch him.

Two days after us, a Swiss boat arrived. An hour later and one of the four crew was at the airport, flying home. All vowed that she would never board a boat again. If that was sailing, she'd done her bit. The motion had become too much for her. She had spent days at the end of the bowsprit in mid-Atlantic asking the sea to take her now. Now! Now!! No one could help her. She threatened to jump if anyone approached. Crazy she might have been, but none of us thought she was mad.

By comparison, no one on *Petronella* reached a life-threatening crisis. If anything, we had enjoyed ourselves. And now, onshore, things were getting better. We did things as a crowd again, made friends as a group again. We could so easily have fallen apart as a crew just then, but we didn't. It took a little while longer for that to happen.

The final crisis, when it came, was a flare-up between Julia and me. The timing was absurd. She was within a week of flying home to California. She was half-living on another yacht at the time, so there was very little by way of detonator for the nuclear meltdown. We were not suffering sleep deprivation or motion abuse. I suppose we were just living in the aftermath of a job completed and challenges fulfilled. Perhaps neither of us was quite ready for the anti-climax of just going home.

The ideal crew

Making a good crew is a different class of problem to the practical ones of keeping a boat in good shape and coping with what the sea and land throw at you. People have their own agendas. They want different things. They are unpredictable. They take your attention when you can least afford to give it. They make life heaven or they make life hell. No wonder people fall in love with boats.

The ideal crew is not for ever singing in the rain and making life for each other happier and more meaningful. That would be the Hollywood Dream-On Crew. It doesn't exist in this world. The ideal crew is the one that has the mix of personalities and interests to minimise the number of suicides and murders, while still getting all the dirty jobs done and not being late for the 3 am watch.

Consider what you are asking of the crew. There is really no reason why relations should get better, the longer people are caged together. You need a strategy to help you cope with this, but the simplest strategy of all – that everyone needs time to themselves off the boat – is only practicable on long sea passages if you order the crew into the liferaft at gunpoint and cut the rope.

You increase your chance of making a good crew by going with the grain of beginnings, middles and ends. I think we were always good at the beginnings. I should have tried to have more beginnings.

The psychology of the crew is symptomatic of and determined by the physical world around them. The ideal crew should not be beaten down by this. They should have the mix of characters and constitutions to support one another through hard times and into the good. But then, the ideal crew does not exist and you must learn to make do with real people.

Crew postscript

When I quizzed Magnus in the Canaries about Julia, I needed to know if his views about her were disinterested. He did not intimate that there was anything between them other than crew comradeship. A year or so after the trip ended they got married.

Magnus's parents told me that he and Julia thought that if I knew about the growing relationship between them after Porto Santo, I would put Julia off the boat. This explained a lot of the oddities in my relationship with them, both in the Canaries and then Africa. It did not, however, explain the bad feeling between myself and Julia during the crossing – that bit of the puzzle is still missing.

Weather

- *I can't forecast weather and nor can anyone else I've met. You can work with most of the weather you'll meet offshore. The rest you just have to live with.*
- *This trip takes you across distinct weather bands. Life becomes a lot easier sailing south of Biscay — warmer, clearer, with the relative comfort of following winds. To call it magic is not overstating it.*
- *You can meet strong winds in any of these weather bands, so always be prepared, but a boat that can cope with Biscay can cope with what comes after.*
- *Light winds can be harder to live with than strong ones. Prepare for these too.*
- *The trade winds may not threaten, but their boisterous charm includes a few nasty habits. Direction may be steady, but strength varies and so do the waves.*
- *Nobody can describe the horrors of rhythmic rolling. Well, there has to be a price for so much pleasure.*

So how do we feel about weather? There are three main types: heavy, light and the stuff in between. The stuff in between is what comes most of the time and gives you good to fabulous sailing. It is what you want to hear being forecast. But any trip of five days or more takes you outside the forecast period and no forecast is so wonderfully accurate that it will be right for where you are at that precise minute.[1] Don't blame a good forecast when you catch something you don't like. A good rule of thumb is to only go to sea in a sturdy boat and be ready for anything, seasonal or unseasonal, from calms to gales.

That said, more than all the things that worried me before we set out was how boat and crew would stand up to the weather. Here we were, setting out on an adventure that would take months to get across the Atlantic Ocean, which would take us so far offshore that distances would be measured in thousands and not hundreds of miles, and where we would have no choice but to take the unknowable conditions of the deep ocean and possibly find that they would test us to the brink of our courage.

The sea did not wait very long before trying us out. We were barely into the Bay of Biscay when the first gale came through to test our mettle and rattle our nerves. After that dusting, we never really looked back for the rest of our adventure.

The weather on this route comes in major bands, and the breaks between are very clear. We had early hints of what it would be like sailing in southern waters as we

---

[1] There are tales of shore-based radio networks where the co-ordinator can work out a forecast for an area of 1 mile radius of where you are. But this is mainly useful when you have a very nasty blow coming up and your very survival depends on getting your tactics right. You will be very unlucky to be facing this sort of thing as you run with the trades to the Caribbean.

picked up the better weather after northern Spain, but it was not until we left Bayona that winter got off our tail. The character of the sailing changed completely heading down to Madeira with the Portuguese trades. This is one of the turning points for wind and current in the Atlantic. The prevailing westerly winds of the north bend southwards and continue to blow south for you until you meet the third and last great wind shift of the north-easterly trades. All this time, moving south, the air and sea is warming and the exposed life on board a little yacht gets easier. On our passage from England to northern Spain we had swapped a sea temperature of about 15°C for one of nearly 20°.

Life gets easier in the south, but don't imagine that the conditions in these great belts of weather always conform to meteorological opinion. Perhaps the weather gods are capricious. Perhaps they haven't read the Admiralty statistics carefully enough. Whatever, there is a lot of variation around the average that I wish I had known more about before we met it.

> We were caught often enough by strong winds at sea as we went our way. I learnt two eternal truths. First, the sea can always blow up a storm when it wants to. Second, I might as well forget about meteorology and just keep practising slab reefing.

Average for Biscay

We learnt a lot from Biscay but, to be fair, we could have learnt most of it while sailing to Cornwall from Sweden, Holland or the Isle of Wight. It just happened that Biscay was our shake-down trip where we learnt whether or not the boat would hang together. Biscay, though, has a dimension that the North Sea and Channel lack. Biscay is ocean sailing. Biscay teaches lessons that can only be learnt a long way offshore, and these are heightened by the Bay's fearful reputation. The lessons weren't all to do with heavy weather sailing. We had lessons to learn about ourselves and doing things offshore.

The trip began well enough, except that sailing hard into a strong westerly so early left us very tired. On the second night we hove-to for a restful night and to start what I thought were good habits for offshore sailing, where crew comfort takes priority over boat speed. Anyway, there was no boat speed against the westerly force 6. Sleep would only cost us a few miles drifting.

The westerly force 2s and 3s over the next few days had us barely south of Ushant when the first gale hit us on our fifth day at sea, but we had our sea legs by now and the build-up to the gale was fun. We stood out on the end of the bowsprit and laughed at the spray in our faces. We photographed the waves steaming in, bright in the sunlight. We marvelled at rain that flattened the sea and left huge rainbows in the western sky. And, most of all, we were happy with the forecast of 5s and 6s. All this fun and nothing really nasty coming our way.

We didn't even feel too bothered when we blew a sail out. The squalls were gusting force 6 and we were late roller furling the genoa. The squall hit and the genoa split along a seam. Then came the gale and it was two days before the wind fell enough to slide the sail out of the roller reefing. By that time, the genoa was like a tattered flag.

The gale gave us about five hours' warning. By then we had three reefs in the main and only the staysail up forward. This gale, like most depressions that track across Biscay, was westerly and we had to sail close-hauled to save our westing. This is the mantra of the Biscay sailor: make west whenever you can.

The waves took a long time to build into a proper Atlantic swell, but by the first morning the confused surface waves had gone and we had 15 footers rolling down on us. We had no anxiety. A lot of water ran on deck, but not many waves were breaking. A few waves swept right over us, coming with a long low hiss before they lashed us and threw water over the cabin roof. The boat would stagger, heel, shake off the water, and then bear away to gather speed before turning back on course. None of us had to touch the tiller. None of us were up there even trying. Mr Monitor would have clambered off the stern into a bunk with us if he could. He might as well, for all the good he was doing. His wind vane gave up wrestling with the tiller and jammed itself right over in a permanent cringe, quite impotent to luff the boat. It made no impression on the rudder until the gale was over.

The boat flew along until night, when we backed the little staysail to slow us for greater comfort. This stopped us slamming but brought us more beam-on to the seas and exposed us to more breaking waves. We still had no feeling of danger. The

Julia on the bowsprit as storm clouds gather.

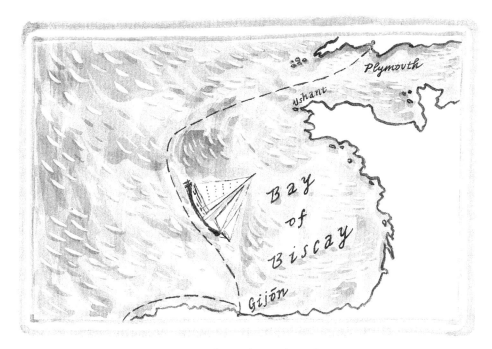

Our route from Plymouth to Gijon.

seas were not doing justice to the wind except in the squalls, when the extra wind instantly raised higher waves.

We were well clear of shipping so we left the boat to sort things out, ran our masthead lights and looked out every half hour or so. I sat up watching more than the others. I wanted to see as much of the gale as I could. I was not planning to sail in many more force 8s.

When the wind dropped to a 6 we shook out a reef and got sailing again. We could not believe it when the second gale started to build just a few hours later. This was more serious but shorter lived, as secondary fronts often are. The seas were perhaps 20 feet, with breaking crests. We dropped the main completely, but even making no more than 2 or 3 knots to windward, we slammed more heavily than before.

The seascape awed us. An endless line of crests and troughs out of the south-west, which the boat rode predictably and easily until some dreadful rogue suddenly stood up and hit us. Rogue waves came in two varieties: an extra-high wave, where two waves in the main train double decked; and the cross-track-nasty, where a low wall of water suddenly rushed at us along the top of, and at right angles to, the main wave.

When two big waves hit us in succession, the first would heel the gunwales under water and the second would push us bodily into that water, so that instead of a stern wake we raised a side wall. From the cockpit we had the novel experience of looking over that wall into the vertical drop beyond it. When night came we hardly bothered with watches. There was little chance of seeing anything and virtually nothing we could do if we did. We pressed on, close-hauled, tiller lashed, making 2 knots under staysail on a lousy course east of south.

After this gale we sailed wonderfully fast for 24 hours under the outer edge of the depression, until the wind died. We dried our gear in the hot sun and went swimming from the dinghy. We were within reach of Spain, but the wrong bit. The storms had pushed us too far east. When we grew weary of the rolling calm we motored for the nearest port.

Crossing Biscay is one of the defining events of this great adventure, even if it is little more than home waters for British and European sailors. You may be lucky and get a fine wind to blow you across. You should certainly time your crossing to get the best wind you can. We knew we were a little bit late. The routing charts showed a noticeably higher chance of gales in September compared to August but, of course, that is just on average. I have seen bad weather there in August. We met a boat in Madeira that left in October and had an easy crossing. Two things come to mind. Don't go too late in the year. Don't let this leg of the journey put you off. An ocean gale is one of the most momentous natural events you can experience under your own steam, and your life is the richer for it. An early gale is also very reassuring – when it's over.

The south is another country

I don't really know where 'the south' began for us, but it was magic. It was like nothing we had experienced in northern Europe.

Once clear of Bayona, and offshore 100 miles, we sailed in a high pressure system with thin, high cloud for most of the time. The wind was so constant from the north that we were nearly caught out by the lesson we had learnt in Biscay: to save our westing at all costs. Now it was such a joy to be broad-reaching under full working sail in easy seas that we were happy to go a long way west, always expecting this direction to be blocked when the wind went south-west or west. I should have looked at the Admiralty routing charts sooner. We found precisely the constant north winds they showed.

What different winds mean to you and your boat depends on your course. For us, the 700 miles from Spain to Madeira was wonderful sailing. The winds varied in strength from flat calm to force 5, but seldom rose more than this. We could make 8 knots with a reefed main and half the genoa in those flat following seas. Even half a gale is almost benign when there is no chill in the sea. The memory of strong winds soon faded and we wished them back when the sails flapped idley, the boat wallowed in the swells, and sleep was disturbed by the crashing of the gear if we tried to run with the mainsail. On two nights we dropped all sail and just drifted rather than suffer following winds that could not keep the main boom out.[1]

---

[1] This is always a problem with heavy gear. The rolling boat spills the wind from the mainsail and the boom comes sliding over. Not even a good preventer can stop the sail and your nerves from fraying, so in the end you drop the sails and strap the boom down into the gallows.

> **Log entry: to Madeira**
> Tonight is incredible. We roll along like a noisy tin can. All clatter and crashes on the inside, but calm and stately outside. It is nearly midnight and the big moon is not up yet. It is pitch-black. The paraffin lamp hangs from the backstay.
>
> The seas push and roll us as they please. Some are just big pussy cats. They threaten but are harmless in the end. Worst are the waves that travel in lines of three. Each in turn rolls us, throwing everything out of order and making tasks 100 times harder. The bigger waves put water into the cockpit, but we roll on sedately into the night.
>
> The lamps in the saloon, turned low, flare as the boat takes a hard knock. I like the soft breeze as the boat rolls and the smell of burning paraffin.

In the main, life in the Portuguese trades gave us our easiest nights and days, made comfortable by our growing certainty that we were done with the hard winds of the north. Nature cannot wish you much harm when the air is warm, the sky has a million stars, and the Milky Way is as clear as a brushstroke on canvas. The late rising of a huge moon meant wonderful stars in the early part of these nights, and near-daylight later on. We set no watches, thinking that we were far enough offshore and outside shipping routes. We saw very few vessels, and then only at night.

Forecasts – well, there's another surprise!

I don't always have a well-informed view of the weather, but then the weather is never an easy thing to predict. I don't just mean that forecasts using linear programs can never be right. Predictive models should either be non-linear or chaotic. Non-linear models have information about the consequences of a change in any one factor as it affects what is happening to *all other factors at that time*. Imagine that. It is theoretically possible, but there is no chance of it in practice as far as anyone with common sense can see. Chaotic models are not even theoretically calculable.[1] No, what I mean is that the weather was never its usual self. No matter where we travelled or what season we were in, the weather even had the locals puzzled by its unreliability.

> In the open anchorage of San Marcos, Tenerife local fishermen forecast a wind shift to north-west which would make the harbour both untenable and impossible to leave. We left and spent a nightmare night at sea, rolling in a flat calm, praying for a strong north-westerly.

[1] There are all sorts of clever things someone could say about the mathematics of chaos and non-linear models but not me, not here, with my brain not even able to work out how to calculate a sun sight.

The south winds we met in the Canaries were at least two months ahead of themselves. This worried us since the pilot books reiterate that harbours there are not safe in southerlies. Even those with a north-facing entrance, like Los Gigantes on western Tenerife, had a backwash big enough to crack us against the pontoons. I know. That was one of the reasons we left that harbour.

We, being new to the Canaries, had the added problem of distinguishing the fierce wind that was unseasonable from the fierce wind that was due to the acceleration zones between the islands. These come as the ocean winds are funnelled between the land. I doubt that they are really predictable at all. I, who had been frightened by the pilot books into losing my casual disregard of weather forecasts, beseeched a port official in Santa Cruz to run his fax and get a forecast for our crossing from Tenerife to Gran Canaria. We would have gone anyway, but we felt great relief to see those wide isobars of high pressure in which no wind could hide. One mile off from Tenerife we hit the acceleration zone and a force 6. A surprise. We romped across to Gran Canaria on a wonderful reach.

These warm winds and warm seas were unthreatening if sometimes uncomfortable. The point is simple: if you have sailed this far you are not likely to be very bothered by these seas. This does not mean that you should relax your guard. The sea will always throw something nasty at you. In the Canaries this is usually when you are in harbour.

Our best guide to the Canaries were our pilot books and I was grateful for them. I worried about the speed of weather shifts and the shelter in the harbours, with good reason. A wind shift can turn a safe anchorage into a surfy lee shore. But I think I had doubled my worries by giving double credence to the pilot books. The cruising yacht coming into a new area supplements the pilot books with 'local knowledge' from other foreign yachts. Beware, this local knowledge may be more up to date and colourful than the pilots, but it is limited, idiosyncratic and often unreliable. Worse, foreign yachts may just give you their interpretation of the pilot rather than tell you what they actually experienced. That's what I mean by double credence.

Leaving the Canaries is a major step for several reasons. Northern European sailors are already far from home, but the next passage is the big commitment – whether it is to Africa or the Caribbean. The weather will have been changeable. Most sailors will take especial care to get a good forecast.

We, of course, had assiduously collected weather forecasts all the way down to the Canaries, though none of this did us much good. Now, leaving the Canaries, we sharpened our interest. We heard forecasts from Madrid, relayed by a local yacht on VHF. Unfortunately, the local weather often seemed unrelated to the wider area synopsis and we lacked faith that Madrid knew much about either. Local fishermen's forecasts and long-stay yachts had us nervously ever ready to shift anchor, but we wanted a more discriminate feel than that for impending bad weather. We turned to the Admiralty routing chart for December. I love these charts, with their immensely detailed records of wind strengths and directions, painstakingly gathered and elegantly presented. I pored over our area with my magnifying glass and carefully sucked up information until the probabilities were certain. As a result, we were completely surprised by the gale that hit us a week later en route to Dakar. It isn't just the locals you can't rely on.

> **Log entry: en route to Senegal**
> The unexpected gale is over. I considered the matter briefly, but decided that it was hardly worth telling the Admiralty to put a new arrow on their routing chart for December.

The steady winds shown by the routing charts only disguised the variation between the averages. We experienced a confusion of winds. We left Gran Canaria on a calm night, so pleased to be at sea that we forgave the wind for dying on us and the night for being so cold. Three hours later a good, honest, sturdy northerly wind-of-the-ocean came at us like a lion. We had all sails set within minutes. Half an hour later, I put in two reefs and dropped the staysail. Half an hour later I had the main and jib down and the staysail back up as our only sail. Sturdy, honest ocean wind, but a tad too much.

The confusion of winds had us reefing and unreefing, ghosting and storming along. Sometimes this was wonderful. We covered 117 miles in one 24 hour period compared to our usual 100. Things went wrong on the fourth day and our trip to Dakar began to look like a bit of a trial. There were long tedious spells of very light winds, even one complete and welcome night of total calm. We had fog at night and haze during the day. This was nothing like the fog of the North Sea, but bothersome now that we were used to brilliantly clear skies. On the sixth day the sky was a single sheet of cloud from horizon to horizon and the wind was a mystery. The barometer for that day tells a good story:

Time	Barometer	Wind	Conditions
0600	974	NE3	
0845	978 – up	None	Becalmed with rain
1145	980 – up	N2	
1600	973 – plummet	N6 or 7	
1800	973 – steady	SE6	
2000	973 – steady	S3	
2200	976 – rising	SE8	Full gale

These wind shifts meant a lot of work. On this day we went from the genoa to working rig of jib, staysail and main; put three reefs in the main for the northerly 6, when running south, and again for the south-easterly 6 when beating south; between 7 pm and 9 pm we put three reefs in the main, shook them out and put them back again; then we dropped the staysail.

At 9.30 pm, with three reefs in the main and the jib up, we were travelling at 6.5 knots, a rare speed for us, and I was crouched in the cockpit watching the dark shapes of dolphins in the waves alongside us and trying to work out how long the gale would last. I ran through 'long foretold etc', but I couldn't work out whether the gale had been developing slowly or had come up rapidly with little warning. My head was rebelling against consecutive thought. It was all irrelevant. No one would get any sleep at that speed, with those waves, and the old main, even triple-reefed, might burst apart.

> **Log entry: gale in the south**
> We ran off the wind to roll the jib away. Magnus brought us gently back on the wind and I went forward to raise the staysail and drop the main. Big seas across the deck soaked me. I hung on till the motion settled down. Up on the roof, clinging to the mast, I see huge waves everywhere, and nothing else. We strapped the boom into the gallows, sheeted the staysail hard, lashed the tiller down, tied the storm light to the backstay, and retired below.

We hove-to that night. The force 8 sometimes seemed like a 9. The seas never built. Sometimes those troublesome three delinquents rolled up, gave us a slapping, rolled us sharply, and poured water over the decks. They were pussy cats compared to Biscay waves. We all slept reasonably well. By morning the wind was force 4, the sky was clear, and the only sign of the gale was the swell.

I don't want to say that gales were an entertainment, because no one should underestimate the power of the sea, but they were wonderfully exhilarating and, after Biscay, we were confident that we could cope with anything less than a severe 9. By now, too, we could reef the main quickly, knew the right sail plans, were happy to heave-to and go below. We had seen enough strong wind to be ready for it. That was never true of the light winds we met.

Becalmings to boast about

Light winds promise peace and quiet, but they deliver wallowing and rolling and untraceable noises. You grow angry with inactivity. You see cat's paws of wind on the sea, but you cannot use it. You try different sails or the engine, or a combination of both, but nothing drives you forward quietly and nothing stops the rolling.

Winds too light for sailing are a war of nerves between crew and boat. In all but the deadest calm, the long, gentle, nearly invisible swell will roll your scuppers under. Peaceful book reading or a snooze on the foredeck are a long wish away. You do what you can to get rid of the worst of the crashing gear and clanking cups, but you are never rid of them altogether. Shock-cord over the plates. Foam pads on drawer stops. In the end the way to peace is like the way to sainthood. Cultivate the patience and attitude of mind to bear these irritants. Try not to get on each other's nerves. No one is having fun.

Light winds are not the same as dead calms. As you travel you will swap notes with other boats about strategies. The big yachts like to keep a steady average speed. Many will motor when boat speed drops below 5 or 6 knots. That, to me, almost negates the nature of sailing. However irritating the elements can be, we came out

After the Biscay storm we sailed wonderfully fast for 24 hours until the wind died. Then we dried our gear in the sun and went swimming.

here to live with them. I had no wish to turn our adventure into a trip around the fuel docks of the Atlantic seaboard. On *Petronella* we didn't have the habit of mind that reaches for the ignition switch when the boat is just ghosting along. Our strategy was simple. We cannot motor across an ocean. When the wind fell to nothing, we were becalmed.

Dead calms are like gales, a force of nature that you can do nothing about. Sitting out a calm is not the same as light weather sailing, just as riding out a gale is not the same as surfing along with two reefs in the main. Between the Canaries and Dakar, 120 miles off Mauritania, we had the calmest becalming I've ever known. The dying afternoon wind raised no waves. By night the sea was a mill pond, and the low swell so long that it soothed us. It was like being on a lake, surrounded by silent land.

A heavy mist made our world silent, still and very tiny. We set watches. A couple of tankers, nothing more, had passed a long way east of us, so we were confident that there was not much shipping about. The watch was spent mainly below, listening for engines. We didn't even bother with a light. Even if we were lit like a Christmas tree no ship would see us till they were too close to miss. If a tanker had come bursting into our little world we would have been hardcore before we could radio to ask if their radar was working.

Two hours after dawn, the sky is heavily overcast and the decks wet with dew. The fog has lifted and a tiny new breeze stirs the sea. The movement gets me out of bed. A noise makes me rush to the companionway. The sea has erupted with a school of dolphins. When they come up together, the whole sea boils. One fellow takes flight, jumping twice at full speed as he chases something. Our close companions roll and swerve, twist and stall, blow and dive in graceful motion, but there is nothing slow about them. They can accelerate away from us without any observable movement of their fins or tails.

I hoist the genoa and we move forward, the dolphins with us. Later, when I hoist the main and we start to make 3 knots, they leave us. Now, an hour later, there is no sign of them. Just the gentle rolling swell and tiny wind ripples under it. Africa is 120 miles east, America is 3000 miles west, but if the haze were to lift I know I would see land and trees and us gliding up some still river.

That dead calm was wonderfully recuperative. Sleep is never easy on a small passage-making boat. The busy days before leaving harbour are tiring. First nights at sea are restless, before you adjust to the timetable of the boat. If you are unlucky, the weather can make sleep hard to come by on those nights. After that, other reasons make sleep elusive. Sometimes it happens that on your night watch the boat sails as gently as a rocked cradle and your shipmates sleep soundly, but on their watches the breeze disappears, little waves and swell do not, and you do not get a worthwhile wink of sleep for the whole six hours. The breeze comes back for your second trick at dawn and you sail into daylight wide awake while the others are back asleep in their pits. Come mid-afternoon your head is strapped tight with iron, your eyes itch with grit, and your skin crawls with fatigue. You lie in your bunk willing the elusive sleep and wondering why your two crew, who are normally so quiet, are now wearing hobnailed boots on deck, speaking through megaphones, and can't steer straight. When the night of total calm comes, sleep.

The ending of any calm is a wonderful release. Hoisting sail to a filling breeze is a magical moment in offshore sailing. The boat steadies as the sails fill, then comes alive. The bow pushes out a new wave, rises to a swell, and comes down with that great 'shuuushing' sound as it shoulders its way forward. You look around for dolphins and then realise it is the boat making these living sounds. You set the sheets and the steering, feel the wind on your face, think about a snack, and forget the cantankerous moments of the calm. It probably never occurs to you that if you had been motoring you would have missed that turning point when the boat and you come alive again.

Is this the trades?

After leaving Africa we sailed straight into the most beautiful northerly 4s to 7s and for the next six days stormed along at 120 miles a day on a beam reach. We had never sailed faster. Speed brought a new tension and mistrust between the three of us on board. I sensed my varmint crew were wondering how to revise their estimate of when we would arrive without me noticing their fraud. And vice versa.[1]

This was not comfortable sailing. Water ran on deck continuously and spray was flung right over us as we rushed at the lumpy seas. We spent one period of 24 hours under triple reefed main and staysail and still made over 6 knots. In the stronger spells we surfed off 15 foot waves. The self-steering loved the wind. Our self-steering problems were all in light winds or when the wave direction was confused. Unfortunately, in this sea area we had some large rogue waves. These would dash in from unlikely angles, rolling *Petronella* 30 degrees one way and then 30 degrees the other, while the self-steering leapt about like a goalkeeper missing penalties. As if that wasn't bad enough, the fickle wind at night played havoc with sleep. If it was strong, we got up to reef. If it was light, we lay rolling in our bunks. It was a tribute to our fortitude that we all took this so well, and the red wine so low.

For most of that first week out of Africa the sky showed all the signs that a huge weather system was building, but this either drifted off to bother somewhere else or came through in unthreatening dribs and drabs. We had two nights of the heaviest squalls of black cloud and rain, but with hardly any wind in them. We were unruffled and didn't bother to drop sail. If any squall had held the wind they threatened, it would have blown our rig away. The fierce rain was a blessing. It washed off most of the red dust of Africa and we hung out our underwear in the evening in the hope of finding it washed, dried and ironed by morning.

Whenever the motion became too much or we started slamming, we adjusted the self-steering to broaden our course. By day three we were roughly due south of and as close to the Cape Verdes islands as we were ever to get, and it occurred to me that we would have had a hard time getting there from Senegal as we had once planned. The pilot book says stay close-hauled after Senegal and the shifting wind will pull you round right to the islands. I think it would, but it would have been a hard, wet and head-banging course to get those 200 miles farther north, and you can bet the current isn't going that way. The better plan would be to visit the islands first, timing your arrival before the trades have set in and make the Cape Verde anchorages uncomfortable. Then take the northerlies to Senegal and Gambia.

---

[1] We always made estimates of how long a journey would take, and sealed these away to be opened on arrival. It was a good way of discussing wind, weather, food consumption and the like, at the beginning of the journey and at any point along it. As for the results, none of us were ever very close to getting it right.

Five days and 600 miles after leaving Africa, when the wind lost most of the north in it, we debated whether this was the trades as though we had had a lifetime of experience in these latitudes. It wasn't. The variable weather between Africa and the trades did not want to let us go. A largish front went through and left 30 hours of near-calm behind it. On day seven, 800 miles from the Casamance, the true trades came as an easterly 6 with just a touch of north. We goose-winged on main and staysail and immediately made over 6 knots due west.

We noted a curious thing at this junction with the trade winds. The air was heavy with red dust, so that our rigging and sails were coated as they had been when we sailed down to Dakar. The dust had the smell of soil and drains too. We were 800 miles offshore.

Ah, there's the rub!

We did not sail into the soft and balmy following breezes of trade wind myth. We had gone farther south than most boats on the trade wind route and had left slightly later, so perhaps our trades were stronger than those usually met by yachts leaving from the Canaries in November and early December.

For a while the following seas remained short and confused rather than the long rollers I had expected. The surface of the sea was completely broken, waves climbing waves everywhere. Changes in the wind strength, up or down, added to this confusion. A squall of force 6 would instantly raise 10–15 foot waves and then leave us with 6–8 foot waves in the force 4 that followed. It wasn't just the surface wind that created strange waves here. About 1200 miles offshore we seemed to sail through a tide race. Waves of 3–4 feet were leaping everywhere and running in all directions. Nothing in the wind accounted for this. A careful plot on the chart showed we were crossing a major depth contour with some isolated peaks, but this was not shallow water. The change in depth was from 3 miles to $2^1/_2$ miles. It seemed odd that changes so far down could have such a strong effect at the surface. The disturbed area of sea was only about 5 miles across, so we swept through in an hour and were back to our usual rolling.

We began experimenting with different sail plans on the very first day of the true trades. At dusk we dropped the main and set the genoa and staysail on opposite sides. This was one version of the classic rig for sailing down the trades. In that force 6 we lost no speed, but the motion became impossibly lively during the night when 8 foot waves from behind had us zigzagging and rolling. There was no comfortable berth on the boat. Even the crew, solid and persistent sleepers normally, couldn't cope.

The next morning we tried another classic trade wind rig. We raised the storm trysail and sheeted it hard amidships to steady the goose-winged headsails. It was hopeless. At first the trysail stole wind from the genoa, so we tacked it onto the other side and let it steal from the much smaller staysail. Our partially blanketed twins were now unstable. With the trysail sheeted tight and almost right on the centreline, the wind went from one side of it to the other as we rolled. Whoop, whoop, whoop went the trysail as it flogged from side to side. The self-steering, which coped better than any of us humans, flung itself about from side to side trying to counter the course changes of the gybing trysail. The boat rolled horribly.

This rig lasted half a day before we went back to one foresail and a boomed-out main. We felt more comfortable. The main tended to dampen the rolling. This was not perfect, but it looked like we were going to stay with it. We were losing our appetite for experiments. It had taken over an hour to take off poles and preventers, run new preventers, re-attach the main, hoist it and set it. We had a feeble gybe, but it still caused one of the preventer line blocks to explode. So we put two preventers on the main.

We never arrived at a soothing solution to downwind sailing in boisterous conditions. The failure of the stabilising trysail was a great disappointment. Twin headsails alone rolled the boat too rapidly and a boomed-out main was vulnerable to hard squalls. Even when there are no squalls it is not relaxing on a dark night 1000 miles offshore to come round into wind to add another reef.

With our preferred rig the biggest danger was in leaving the mainsail up too long before reefing. We did some crude calculations. We reckoned that if the trades never blew as hard as a Biscay gale, we could put two reefs in the main and leave it up in all conditions. What we were really calculating was whether we could safely leave the main up all night. It seemed feasible. I mean, it seemed feasible at the time we did the calculations, but when we had to turn the boat into wind to put in the necessary two reefs we immediately revised our estimate of wind strength from 4 to top end 6.

Downwind sailing is deceptive for three reasons. First, the boat seems capable of coping with a lot of wind from behind because this point of sailing is easier on your body. Second, the wind strength that you perceive is reduced by your boat speed through the water. Turn to windward and it is increased by this speed. Third, in the trade winds most of your estimates will be made while lounging in the cockpit, arranging body bits to keep the tan even. This is where you live unless you go up on deck to check the rigging and stare meaningfully at the set of the sails. You will get a different sense of wind strength when you go forward. On *Petronella*, the wind fair hustles through the gap between mainsail and staysail. A force 3 in the cockpit can feel like a 5 on the foredeck. I sometimes scurried back without raising sail, frightened by the half-gale up there.

On this day, as we prepared to double reef, this was no pussy cat sea. The waves were travelling fast, about 12 feet high. It felt like riding a mountain ridge, with huge views to either side. Nature could take us any time it chose. Instead, Nature played a little joke on us.

Julia and Magnus were to do the sail handling as we put this reef in. When we were all ready to turn to windward, Julia went to the end of the bowsprit to be clear of the staysail boom and Magnus stood at the mast. I was easing the boat to windward when suddenly we were nose-diving into a wall of water twice as tall as Julia. I yelled, 'Here's a big one!' Magnus looked up and yelled. Julia was looking back at us. She never saw what hit her. About 5 tons of salty water. The boat stopped almost dead. The tiller tore out of my hands. I grabbed it back and it flung me over the cockpit. I thought it was going to snap. Then I had control again and we were all laughing.

'What was that?!' Magnus and I were saying. 'Did you see it, Julia?'

Julia had been wondering why she could see so much sky behind the steering vane when she was suddenly up to her waist in solid water and being squashed by a huge wave. She wasn't sure if there was still boat under her feet.

This was a foretaste of our early days in the trades. By that evening we were running in a force 7 with 15 foot waves regularly coming past. We put a third reef in the main and went on even faster. The waves came in steadily from the east with double-decker monsters every ten minutes or so. The stern rose comfortably, but the decks ran constantly. The roll of the hull put the bulwark under, then back she came on course, steady for another ten minutes or so. The sea outside the hull was whooshing by.

Milk Run?

Early evening, force 7 . . . 15 foot waves breaking for as far as we can see. Three reefs in the main . . . running fast . . . decks awash . . . waves twist us . . . the stay-sail flaps and slams onto its preventer. It's like a noisy fairground ride. Inside, we tense in anticipation. Waves hit the turn of the bilge like a bomb going off next to my head. Outside, the sea is almost roaring. I thought it was the Forties that roared. Have we sailed into the Roaring Twenties by mistake? This wasn't in the glossies about trade wind sailing.

Safety harnesses tonight. No riding the bowsprit tonight. No running forward to collect flying fish. Just staying clipped on in the cockpit to reach the tiller in case we gybe.

Resting or trying to sleep down below was a torment. The most stable position was flat on our backs, holding tight to the ties of the lee cloths, but our internal organs had no handholds. They accelerated and decelerated with the boat, at a different rate to the body. Lying on the side gave them less distance to gather speed, but then the body had to tense every muscle to wedge itself against bulkhead or lee cloth. Neither position was conducive to sweet dreams. Deck was the place to be. No wish for sleep there. We could feel the amazing life of the boat as we surged forward. The power of the sea is impressive, but the ability of a small boat to cope is even more so. Mankind has not been wasting its time for the last few millennia. It has made little sailing boats that can run like hounds before these seas.

A crossing of two halves

Of course the trade wind crossing wasn't all stormy and uncomfortable. It was just a surprise. The strong winds we got from our southerly route suited us. They allowed a very much faster crossing than we had originally planned. *Petronella* is slow, but she is remarkably robust and can carry a good wind. It happened by chance that we took her down to where the wind blew longer and stronger.

We really did run for days without touching the sheets.

All this changed halfway across. Winds that had been growing stronger, with bigger squalls at night, suddenly lightened and we sailed into those cloudless blue skies of travellers' tales.

The log entries show we became more chirpy. There were several reasons for this: our morale probably rose when the weather began to fit our expectations – a bit more certainty at sea is no bad thing; after the boisterous stuff we felt completely confident of handling softer weather; this steadier weather was worth a lot in more restful and longer sleeping. A crew may sail on its belly, but it sleeps on its back in a bunk, which it likes to be calmer than a bucking bronco.

This second half required much less deck work. We really did run for days without touching the sheets. Reefing was a memory. This was restful for the mind as well as the body. Coming up into the cockpit, the first question was not, 'What sail changes are needed?' but 'Where did I leave that novel?' We grew lethargic. Apart from moving between sun or shade we only had cooking, cleaning and stitching to do. If it had not been for the exercise of perpetual bracing and balancing against the rolling, our muscles would have wasted away. Ironically, then, the mainsail decided to tear.

There was no particular reason for the mainsail to split except old age. The wind was a pleasant force 4 and the sail was held firmly and not flapping. I heard a 'chuuuf' sort of noise and looked up to see a long rip in one of the upper panels just getting longer. It seemed better to lose a sail in those easy conditions than many others I could think of. We changed the sail and went on our way as before, in near-total lassitude.

This easier weather also brought back the full pleasure of balmy nights at sea. The night air was warm enough to sit up in just a tee-shirt and there was no need to hide from spray even though the boat still bustled along. Little squalls still came regularly, but we were never over-canvassed. All that was missing from a trade wind idyll were dolphins. We saw none in these softer winds.

Full speed ahead on the last lap

Even lovely soft winds outgrow their welcome. The closer we got to the Caribbean, the more we just wanted to arrive. Daily runs of 105 miles were frustrating after the 125 and 130 of the first two weeks. The weather caught our mounting excitement. The force 5s and 6s came back about 400 miles from Trinidad & Tobago. As our daily runs rose into the 110s, tension on board reached screaming point. Who wins the prize for guessing the crossing time? Sadly, some of us knew already that the estimate sealed in the envelope back in Africa was wrong. But I wasn't letting on to them and they weren't letting on to me.

It would have been an anticlimax to have poodled up to a Caribbean island in a whisper of a wind. We wanted to arrive in a rush. But the return of the better winds added a particular thrill. Imagine this: at the noon of a day you know that you have 150 miles still to go, and that you can do it before dusk tomorrow. A close-run thing, to be sure, but possible. Now we had the pilot book out for real. There was no question of entering Scarborough, the main port of Tobago, in the dark. There are shallows off the entrance, and who knows whether the channel buoys will be as marked. The waning moon did not give enough light for tricky pilotage and the fast current round the south end of the island could too easily push us onto the reefs there. Crossing an ocean does not make you a better inshore pilot. We bit our nails and hoped the wind would not fail us. Nothing can express the anticipation of knowing, with all that ocean now behind you, that you could be in harbour tomorrow night.

A matter of fine judgement was whether we might have to stand off for a night to enter harbour in daylight. With this wind and current I reckoned that a prudent distance for heaving-to could be around 40 miles off Tobago. Can you imagine what this means? To someone who cut his sailing teeth on the Thames estuary and North Sea, 40 miles off is a bit like still sitting in the pub car park. I didn't dare heave-to in less than this in case the GPS was giving us a wrong position. But what if I got it wrong, hove-to this far offshore, and then woke to a flat calm? Heaving-to for one night was not going to be a popular decision. But if it led to the next night at sea as well, mutiny would be pleasant compared to what the crew might have in store for me.

A long way from Thames, Dover and Dogger Bank

We never got the hang of weather forecasting in the trades. With no radio forecasts, we relied on our knowledge of meteorology. We all had a go at reading the books on board and interpreting their illustrations, and Julia even sketched the skies so we could have a record of previous days, but our best bet was rapid response to rising fear rather than forward planning and prediction.

We had signs of big bad weather more often than we had bad weather itself. We might have misinterpreted the signs because the weather was often not at all what we had been expecting. Instead of blue sky and sea we often had heavy cloud. The mornings were very grey before the sun burned the night cloud away. Daytime cloud was welcome. Without it, the sun would have shrivelled us.

> **Log entry: day 12**
> Something big is building. Low, white, fluffy clouds come out of the east at speed. Above them, long streaky clouds run north to south across their track like the high clouds that foretold gales in Biscay. The new swell has a touch of north. This could be our first big blow of the crossing. The 6s so far have not troubled us.
>
> We double reef the main at dawn. If it looks like a full gale we'll run under staysail alone.

No two days were alike, even if the difference between them was just a bit more or a bit less wind, a bit more or a bit less swell. The wind and swell kept coming and I think we could all manage to predict that we would not run out of either. In the early days of our crossing we thought that the wind would drop away at night. It did not. If anything, it seemed to increase and our squalls came mainly at night. We shortened sail at dusk to save having to do it in the dark, but these night squalls were never enough to over-power the boat. On some nights they came through at half-hour intervals. Between the squalls the wind was so light that we were impatient for the next squall to arrive. The strongest winds often came just around dawn and lasted till midday. At their best they had us surfing down waves, as far as *Petronella* can manage that trick.

No one told me it would be this bad

Earlier I told you that the first lesson we learnt was that sailing in the south was a new experience in pleasantness. The second lesson was that running down the trades can also be truly, truly unpleasant. This is not the awfulness of the blustery wind and burning sun, or of drinking another warm beer or finishing the last decent novel on board. It isn't even the awfulness of crawling into those bed sheets for yet another night. It is the rolling.

When we dropped anchor in Tobago the overwhelming relief we all felt was that the rolling was over. Nothing I had read, no one I had spoken to, had prepared me for how bad it would be. The heart of this is rhythmic rolling. All boats on a dead run are inclined to roll because the main driving sails do not press the hull over firmly and the waves and winds can sneak around the stern of the boat and give it a bit of a sideways shove. I have never cared for the rolling motion of a dead run.

From my first experiences of sailing I have hated downwind approaches into rivers or harbours, even when getting there involved slogging into the wind. That turn onto a queasy run felt as though the sea hadn't quite let go of you; might or might not let you arrive safely. I hated that sensation, but not with the passion that I came to hate rhythmic rolling.

> **Log entry: day 18**
> It is odd that the motion no longer disturbs our sleep. It disturbs everything else. As soon as I got out of my bunk I was being flung about the boat, and even simple tasks like making coffee may end in a messy floor. We roll heavily. Not quick dinky little rolls, but full-blooded affairs where first one deck is rolled under and then the other. Every 10 to 15 minutes a huge roll occurs, and whatever you are doing just has to wait. The term 'rhythmic rolling' insinuates itself into my mind. Did I invent it or just remember it? Whatever, it's bloody awful.

I do not know the physics of rhythmic rolling so I can't explain it to you. I can only describe it. The core of the matter is that the movement of the boat gets more extreme from one roll to the next. The rolls gradually worsen over a period of about ten minutes until the hull can't roll further or more violently. There is a final, massive, neck-wrenching roll that threatens to throw everything off the boat that isn't strapped down. Then the hull springs upright and stops rolling. All the massive energy has been dissipated. The boat sails on, quiet now for a few minutes. Then it begins to roll again.

There is nothing you can do except hang on while the boat gets through its crisis. The nerve-wracking thing for us on board was that life now reduced to the 10- or 15-minute period of the rhythmic roll. We could attempt nothing that couldn't be completed in the period before the final huge heave. All tasks, from cooking to reading to walking to sleeping, got reduced to stages able to be completed before we gave both hands and all other body parts to the job of hanging on. The mind focused on this to the exclusion of all else. Conversations were broken-backed affairs that ran down to sporadic phrases as the crisis neared, and picked up briefly afterwards. The body thought ahead, shutting out all other concerns except being next to a stout handhold for that final roll. Love, hate, fear, anger, lust, thirst and hunger all took on a 15-minute pulse. Serenity, contemplation, spirituality and charity all disappeared from the lexicon. This was not a time for pastel shades. Verse was not whispered. Crudities and curses were screamed.

We could never forecast the conditions for rhythmic rolling. Whatever made the difference between the usual awful rolling, and the murderous, suicidal upgrade to rhythmic rolling was too subtle for us. Some days we had it. Other days we didn't. Nor did we know what ended the rolling. After a few hours or a few days of nightmare the world suddenly lightened up and we realised that the rhythmic rolling had stopped. Our minds could again grapple with the life and death questions of lunch and dinner, one cockpit cushion or two.

Of course we tried to stop the rolling. We changed our sailing course relative to the wind, hoping that a bit more of a reach with both sails on the same side would dampen the roll. Perhaps we didn't take this far enough. I mean, we were still trying to get to Trinidad & Tobago and some of our desperation course shifts had us pointing at Bermuda. We rolled the genoa in or out, hoping that a change in speed would make the difference, but there was usually wind to spare and our speed would probably not have dropped much unless we went under bare poles and dragged warps. Which we never did. I mean, by now we reckoned that the best solution to rhythmic rolling was to reach land, and we were not likely to hang about in mid-Atlantic with warps, buckets and old car tyres straining our stern cleats.

We were not the only boat to suffer. I am sure that every boat on the trade wind route gets rhythmic rolling, to a greater or lesser degree. Most of the accounts I have read talk about severe rolling, and most of the other sailors I

The weather was never far from our minds — even to the point of providing bedtime reading.

met had tales to tell of it. The two boats that arrived in Tobago closest to us had suffered. On both boats at least one member of the crew had been crazy enough to want to end the experience in death. Both boats had sailed under twin headsails only. The third boat in harbour when we arrived said they had not suffered rhythmic rolling. Perhaps not. This was a beautiful sailing hull and might have been designed especially for running downwind in big following seas. I don't know. Alternatively, their good fortune might have been because this sleek hull flew a single small jib all the way across, kept up to the north, and took 28 days on the short route from the Canaries.

When something affects your life as fundamentally as rhythmic rolling it is hard not to conclude that it must have had a deep impact on the way we behaved towards each other. It certainly had explicit effects on other boats we met. Odd, then, that I missed this when I was so sensitively worrying about crew psyche. Perhaps we didn't admit to this exogenous effect because of our British phlegmatism and stoicism. Hmmm. If so, it must have been doubly hard on Julia, an American.

Navigation and seamanship

♦ *GPS makes you competent and gives you comfort. Don't think of going without it.*

♦ *Carry a sextant just in case. But carry a spare GPS so you never need the sextant.*

♦ *Adopt good practices for using GPS, to appease the purists.*

♦ *Have windvane self-steering and learn to live with it. Self-steering is what gives you back your life.*

♦ *You can be flexible about keeping night watches or not, but in the end your life depends on them. There is more shipping out there than you ever see.*

♦ *Not all the gear you take will be useful but it is difficult to predict which is and which isn't. Some little things add immensely to comfort, independence and, therefore, safety.*

We should see land by now

We could not have made this journey so easily, accurately and confidently without GPS. I never want to go back to the uncertainties of pre–electronic position fixing. Some sailors may have misspent their youth mastering the sextant or the Viking star stick or the flight path of seagulls or whatever, but this is not for you or me. I am prepared to argue that not carrying GPS when it is so cheap, simple and accurate is the most irresponsible thing a small–boat sailor can do.

For the first time we must find a tiny speck in the ocean rather than a great lump of continent. We thought we saw Madeira, but we were looking at Porto Santo.

After eight idyllic days, there on the horizon, dead ahead, were three tiny peaks of land. It had to be Madeira. The GPS said that we were 70 miles away. What does any island look like from such a distance? An hour later a darker line of cloud separated itself from some white fluffy ones and the small island of Porto Santo resolved itself into a single small piece of land with the darker mass of Madeira to the west. Good timing. An hour later, the sun set spectacularly and our landfall after eight days became invisible under black rain clouds. We stood the first night watches for a week.

This is a book about your ocean crossing, but GPS is something for all yachts in all types of waters. By the time you have tired of sailing around some lesser seas and are ready for the ocean, you should have had plenty of experience with GPS.

Navigation tasks usually have to be done down below. On some boats in all conditions, and on all boats in some conditions, looking up navigation data like tides and lights with your head over the chart table can turn into an exercise in sensory deprivation if it goes on longer than five minutes. Fast and brain-free navigation at sea is not a luxury. Getting an accurate plot on the chart should not reduce anyone's thinking power to that of a mashed potato and nor should it take them away from handing, reefing and steering.

What I learnt out on the ocean is that my little electronic GPS box of tricks can make these long offshore passages as simple as driving up a motorway. Simplicity is a good aim to have. I was already a fully practising user of GPS at the outset, but I remained a closet admirer of the mysterious sextant. My full intellectual, spiritual and emotional conversion to GPS came on the day I tried to teach the crew the wonders of the sextant.

No more index errors

I have carried two sextants ever since I got *Petronella* and have waited for the right moment to try them. Halfway across the Atlantic I got down Mary Blewitt's succinct book on astro-navigation and reminded myself of the theory and practice of sun sights. The crew looked interested, but after ten minutes went back to their own affairs. They did not notice that three hours later I was turning Mary's pages in deep confusion. I was trying to reconcile Mary's method with another, which ten years ago I had thought simpler. Ten years, two sets of terms for almost the same measurement. The longer I tried to reconcile these slight differences, the more total my confusion became.

It was afternoon when I emerged on deck. I explained to the crew about index error and how to calculate it; the sun's declination and how to measure it; the proper grip for the sextant, and how to hang onto the deck at the same time. I then found that the afternoon sun was out of sight from the only place where I could wedge myself and still have two hands free for the sextant. I'd had enough by now.

When I came up next morning it was for action, not more book learning and confusion. It took me an hour just to fiddle with different filters for sun and horizon and get an acceptable value for index error. I took five sights, and Julia recorded the times and angles for each. Then Magnus took five. Then I spent an hour trying to work the data into a position line.

I describe this because of the reaction of the crew. They are not of the sextant generation. They had never even seen one. They had just sailed 4000 miles knowing all the while where they were to within a couple of hundred feet, and now what they wanted to know was what was so wrong with GPS that I wanted to spend all this time getting a single line that could not itself fix our position, and was anywhere from $1/2$ a mile to 3 miles wrong. Or more. I was a bit rusty on the essential arguments to persuade them that the crudities of bringing a mirror image of the sun down to an uncertain horizon on a boat rolling through 30 degrees was well worth the single line of dubious accuracy you got from the pen and paper and headsplitting mental arithmetic that followed. I did my best. I failed.

I shall continue to carry sextants and books and hope to make this work when I have to. I may, like other navigators, become addicted to sextant sights. But not yet. Sextant navigation is the very last resort for my type of sailing. The true fallback for my GPS is a portable GPS, tried, tested and stowed in a waterproof, shock-proof, lightning-proof container.

Get yourself a sextant if you haven't got one. This must be a good time to buy. I imagine the second-hand market is over-supplied. But don't bother using it. You have enough anxiety without wondering where you have been and where you are going.

I know my comments on GPS will upset some who call themselves purists, so here is a proviso. No one should rely on a fix from any form of navigation instruments to the exclusion of common sense. I know that official advice is not to rely on GPS when within 3 miles of land in the Caribbean because of errors in recording old-fashioned chart data and various interferences to the satellite signals. Certainly not. Use your eyes as well. But the cocked hat of three hand-bearing compass sightings can put you 3 miles wrong without even trying. Offshore on the ocean, 3 miles is pretty trivial. Ask the sextant purist who takes issue with me how good they felt when closing land after four weeks at sea and three days of heavy clouds. Overcast skies are more common than 33 yearly meteor storms.

Beware the human errors

We did not mindlessly accept the numbers our GPS gave us because the GPS might have given back some garbage that we had fed into it. It is very easy to mis-key the latitudes and longitudes of waypoints[1]. We usually checked one another's entries. Any error that we didn't pick up this way usually got noticed once it was time to take a serious interest in the waypoint. Also, some of the information that the GPS offered was less reliable than other bits. We regarded the speed and direction readings as a joke. I mean, we used to watch the GPS tell us that we were travelling on a steady course at a couple of knots when we knew we had not even dragged the anchor for the last four days. This, then, meant we only chose to use certain functions of the GPS; there was always the danger that the GPS had got lost but was too embarrassed to tell us. This may not happen so much with GPS but it did with Decca, so we routinely checked each fix to see if it looked right. And we plotted all of them.

Our main source of navigation error was transcription, writing down the wrong latitude and longitude of the fixes. We saw some weird positions on the earlier legs of the journey. Out in mid-Atlantic it was not so easy to spot such errors. Then it became important to always record a position in the written log, so that we could backtrack and check any unlikely marks on the chart.

Human error is something to guard against, but not in the way I have heard from some purists. They would do away with GPS because its ease and simplicity induce sloppy-mindedness in the navigator. I can't agree. Too much ease and simplicity? That's the kit for me. To be lulled into a sense of comfort by staggeringly

[1] This is a key concept in using GPS. A waypoint is simply a useful place on your journey – a place you left, want to go to, or avoid. You tell GPS the co-ordinates of the waypoint and it tells you where you are relative to that place.

consistent accuracy. Let me be lulled, O Lord, and let it be now. In this ocean of uncertainty, let me have a position I can trust and, if not trust, at least check against a line of ones I do trust. Let the purists put on hair shirts. I'd rather wear metaphorical carpet slippers in my navigatorium.

GPS has so many standard functions that not all are useful on this type of journey. Our favourites were few in number and easy to learn: position, waypoints, speed, course, time to arrival and from departure point. We were wary of anything that seems to invite blackbox-type errors. We also avoided over-automating our routine functions. Practice in use helps to maintain accuracy. For both reasons we never bothered to link waypoints into routes.

The fourth crew member

On a three-person boat the fourth crew member is usually the self-steering, but GPS was more part of our social life. We all heard those friendly 'beep beeps' that marked the end and beginning of each night watch. The off-going person switched the GPS on to record our position and heading. They then switched it off, and the on-coming person usually turned it back on to see what it said. Position was again checked part-way through the watch. The little 'beep beep' woke me when I was off watch, but I loved it. I knew the crew was about ship's business. I'm a nervous man. I sleep better for that knowledge.

We have no time to stand and steer

My rule of thumb was to assume in all our manoeuvring and sail setting that we were singlehanding. That way, we were always able to cope with just one person active at a time. This was only possible with self-steering. This is such vital gear and so continuously in use that our relationship with it was one of love and hate. No equipment could reach the pitch of perfection we sometimes demanded of it.

Self-steering is a near-living thing, sensing the wind and water around it and responding to their forces. It only performs as well as the rest of the boat allows it. It only works well when sails and course match the wind and sea conditions, and these are only right when the crew get off their deck cushions and do it. Our relationship with the self-steering was almost humanistic. So of course we cursed it. Self-steering can be more stubborn than a mule if you treat it badly.

No windvane self-steering will keep the boat on a set course other than to the wind, and that is what you must live with on your adventure. Compass courses are for the big ships, who need give nothing away to wind and sea. On a little sailing boat the fickleness of the wind even over an hour makes a nonsense of a compass course. Over a week or three the sensible approach is to stay on the best point of sail in roughly the right direction until you are a day or two away from your destination, and then home in on it. Even then, don't think that you or your crew can keep a better course than the self-steering. Forget all those moments when you glance at the compass and see a bad course. The vital ability of self-steering is to steer a better average than you.

Another day of quiet winds. I am intently watching the self-steering gear as the seas twist our stern and roll us about. Despite working so hard, Mr Monitor steers us west. I wonder whether to adjust the tiller lines, but since no one has made any adjustment to the vane or touched the tiller for the last three days, I won't break with tradition now.

We would not only work harder if we were hand-steering, but also suffer all sorts of extra difficulties. On dark nights, with no easy way of watching the wind direction, we would oscillate between wild over-corrections, ranging from gybe to broad-reach, while always being off course. Not clever for a boat goose-winging with preventers. Mr Monitor doesn't needs a telltale to know which way the wind blows.

The type of self-steering you choose can have a great effect on other aspects of your sailing. It was only much later, when I was rethinking why we had not used twin foresails for our trade wind rig, that I wondered if it had something to do with the self-steering. We made the mainsail the heart of our rig because it seemed most comfortable going downwind and because running with the main followed naturally from the broad reach we had on leaving Africa. If we had heeded the textbook and adopted twin foresails, we might have gone the full hog and steered by jib sheets tied to the tiller. If this balance between jib sheets had proved an effective form of steering, we might have remained under twins. You might like to try it on your own ocean crossing. Personally, I am naturally a lethargic sailor and can't do with this messing with sails and lines, so when we saw the mainsail working well and the twins not, I was easily persuaded to stay with the main.

Steady as you go, Mr. Monitor.

Two other factors influenced me. First, why swap the late twentieth-century technical advances of the Monitor for an antediluvian hit-and-miss pair of jib sheets? Second, sailing under twins does not stop the awful rolling, and that was our main reason for keeping the mainsail up. I have read accounts of other crossings when the moment of joy at the pure simplicity of self-steering under twin foresails gives way to grumping about the dreary, weary, never-ending, white-knuckle hanging on of rhythmic rolling.

Log entry: day 15

Most small-boat sailors love the sense of being part of nature that comes from having to use the wind and currents. Without thinking too much, most identify with the great days of sail over the last three centuries. Perhaps this is a blinkered view. Perhaps the technical perfection of self-steering and electronic navigation on modern yachts radically removes them from the enormously active, purposeful sailing of those tall ships as they explored, traded, fished and fought. If we were not so Western-centric we might see that modern technology makes us more like the ancients who half-sailed, half-drifted across the vast oceans in rafts like *Kon-Tiki* and *Ra*.[1]

Today, as Julia and I sat stitching on the foredeck while Magnus concocted a new dish of sweet and sour onions and bean burgers with rice, the boat moved 30 miles west. We do not navigate. Not really. We record progress since we last looked at the GPS. We do not steer. Not really. Mr Monitor takes the boat closer to our destination. We get on with life.

Self-steering, whether hi- or low-tech, is not about steering. It's about giving you back your life. This seems like a good deal to strike, and you can lose out on this by striving for super-accurate electronic steering that requires you to run the engine daily, service the stern gland weekly, and wash the casing in soapy water every Thursday. What is better still is that the life the self-steering gives you back is better than the one you had in the beginning. It gives you a life on the ocean, then it gives you a life that is part of the ocean.

Watch out

A most serious question for a shorthanded crew is whether to stand regular watches at night. Not all the pros and cons of standing night watches carry the same weight. Night watches can deprive you all of the best hours of sleep, and leave the crew permanently tired. Conversely, not keeping watches on an ocean passage can leave the crew without enough activity to make them healthily tired, while the anxious skipper never gets more than half an hour with his head down.

---

[1] The expeditions of Thor Heyerdahl attempted to demonstrate that earlier civilisations had been able to cross oceans in balsa rafts and reed boats. Given the small sail areas and water-logged hulls, those vessels went with the weather and current, and the skipper probably had the same indifference to navigation that I have.

Keeping watches gives everyone the chance to see the night skies and guarantees undisturbed time with their own thoughts. Not everyone welcomes this.

The benefits of keeping night watches vary with the sea conditions and your location. It is sensible to be flexible and not stand watches some nights if it fits the circumstances, or just let people keep watch intermittently. We did all these things, but our prevailing attitude to night watches changed as our journey progressed. I stopped seeing watches as a way to keep the crew occupied and instead saw them as the difference between life and death. I may be overstating matters a little. Or not.

> **Log entry: towards the Canaries**
> We've stood watches every night so far and we need to get better at it. We had an easier time across Biscay and then to Madeira because we all slept at night. Now we are tired, not yet into a routine. The message is clear for our ocean crossing: a crew of three keeping full night watches must spend more of the day sleeping.

The night watch is special. You have the boat to yourself, to watch the sky and sea, or just let your mind drift in a way that the bright light of day does not allow. Perhaps waking introspection is as necessary to our well-being as the dreams of sleep. In the south the conditions were ideal for night sailing. We could sit in the cockpit with just a light shirt for warmth. Most of the time the sea stayed where it should and didn't come on board to embrace us. The stars far offshore were wonderfully bright, and I never tired of watching the night sky. But most of all, there was the moon.

When we sailed with half-moons, they left the sky to the stars. The full moon gave way to nothing. I had never seen such rising moons as those around Madeira. The rising full moon came over the horizon as big and as golden as the sun. A more primitive and ignorant mind than my own would have sworn it was a second sun. The silver light only came when the moon was well clear of the horizon, and then it lit the whole world. It gave enough light to read by. We barely needed navigation lights and sometimes just ran with a paraffin light in the rigging.

> **Log entry: towards Madeira**
> Sailing by moonlight bright as day. We keep no watches. The crew sleep. Julia wakes to check a reference in a book and eat a cracker with me. Magnus sleeps and wakes and mutters. I look out when I remember, but soon I will be asleep too. The paraffin lamp hangs from the backstay. A small boat might see our light at half a mile, if they are keeping a good watch. A big ship would only see us on radar.

Night sailing, though not to be missed, is not reason enough to keep night watches. Initially, in Biscay, we did not bother with night watches because of the very bad weather, which made keeping watches rather pointless, and then because of the not-so-bad weather, which tired us and made us need more sleep. We were also following what had worked for me once before when sailing Biscay – when

Sailing by moonlight, bright as the day.

comfort beat speed, and safety barely figured at all. Having chosen this tactic once, the agenda was set. We kept no night watches until we had good reason to.

On our passages down to Africa we set night watches only according to weather and position. When the wind was strong, we stood guard against a gybe. When the wind was light, we dropped all sail and slept. When land was coming up, we kept watch. Far offshore, we did not. We did of course look out for ships, but saw very few. If we had thought ships were passing, we would have stood watches. But we didn't, so we slept.

Formal watches or not, I never slept right through a night. When I woke I went up the companionway stairs and looked around. I did it for the pleasure of seeing the night, but I also looked around for ships – as I would during the day. We all did this to some degree. These informal night watches confirmed our view that there was very little shipping about.

By the time we were ready to leave Africa we had a policy. Once offshore, we would only keep night watches when needed. The only reasons to keep night watches at sea are weather, other vessels, or icebergs. Nothing else. There may be other things to hit in the deep ocean, like whales and logs and floating containers, but these are random events and don't carry lights. A person on watch will only see them by chance. There may be other things to guard against, such as a rigging failure or burst seacock, but if you set night watch for this you should have done more maintenance before you set out.

Our conclusion about not keeping night watches was the same as most people's. Even those who had kept watches all the way down to the Canaries and Africa were not planning to keep watch on the crossing. Most written accounts say the same. I suppose there is safety in numbers, just as getting run down always happens to someone else. We had plenty of clichés to support our thinking.

So much for clichés and policy. After leaving Africa we never had a night without watches. Four things account for this:

♦ The weather was so boisterous and variable for the first week, and threw up such slamming seas, that we immediately had to stand watches. Then, after we picked up the trades we were running, and felt too vulnerable to leave the tiller unwatched for long. By the time we got used to the trades and confident of not gybing, we had other reasons to keep night watches.
♦ Lethargy and boredom. We needed something to burn off our energy.
♦ I wanted us all to stay in touch with the boat and the tasks of sailing. Standing proper watches was my way of making sure we did. It was very much my own view rather than one I discussed with the crew. I would have raised it with them but the fourth factor had kicked in after only a few days at sea.
♦ We nearly got run down by a fishing boat.

A fine kettle of fish

It was our third night, we were 300 miles from Africa and 200 miles south of the Cape Verde islands. We had seen no ships since leaving and I thought we were done with shipping. When Magnus called me on deck I could see a large, ocean-going fishing boat no more than half a mile away. We were sailing at 5 knots and the ship was doing about 8. It was getting bigger very fast on a direct collision course. We had all our deck and mast lights on. Tricolour, bicolour, steaming and spreader. The ship obviously hadn't seen us.

> **Log entry: day 4**
> Magnus was on watch. He woke me at 5 am. 'There's something you should see,' he said, and went back to the main hatch. I found my underpants easily enough, but knew I was in trouble when I got both feet through the same leg, and was too confused to know which way round or up the pants were. Magnus was not impressed.
> 'You don't need them. Just hurry up.'
> He began to explain the urgency as I staggered up into the cockpit.
> 'It's been on a constant bearing for ages, but because I could see the red light I thought it would pass ahead of us.'
> Dead ahead of us, on a converging course, were two white lights and a red. Plus enough deck lights to floodlight a football stadium.
> 'I thought it was a very large ship a long way off, but it's a smaller ship really close.'

Magnus sensibly wanted to gybe, but I was trying to figure out which way was best and how to make the ship aware of us. I thought it might accidentally or deliberately follow us round. I asked Magnus to shine the half-million candela Megabeam at the ship, and while he was plugging that in I prepared preventers and sheets to gybe.

We shone the huge beam of light straight at the bridge, but the ship kept coming. Its bow, clear in our light, rose and fell massively in the swell. It would break us in two if it fell on *Petronella*, and all they would know of us would be some bits in the trawl net. I was sheeting in for the gybe when the ship began to turn away. I gybed anyway. We were 100 yards away and I wanted a lot more than that. I didn't want to be caught if they turned back. We ran off to the south for half a mile and then came back on course to the west. The fishing boat was a mile away and we would cross its stern.

I was more shaken by this near-miss than the many others in my career. Partly because it happened so quickly, with me half-asleep, weak from some flu-like bug and anxious about a leaking hull fitting. More, though, this fishing boat was not behaving like others I have met. Fishing boats on Dogger Bank and in Biscay have often come close to *Petronella*, turned round, and an hour later been back on our tail, but I have become sure that they always knew where my boat was. A flash of a light was always enough to turn them away. I had no confidence in this ship. We had no evidence that they were keeping watch. They had not responded to the lights Magnus had switched on before calling me. If they had radar, and if it worked, and if it was switched on, then no one had looked at it in the last half-hour. *Petronella* gives a reasonable radar reflection, even in those lumpy seas.

Nor was I very happy about sinking just here. This blind ship would be no help if it rammed us and there was no traffic compared to the North Sea or Biscay. If *Petronella* sank, our liferaft would travel west with the wind and current, to a shore more than 2000 miles away. Even Biscay gives you more hope than that.

Two points emerge from this. One about watch keeping on our boat. The other about watch keeping on the opposition. What saved us was our watch keeping, not theirs. Magnus had seen that ship long before it closed on us. It only got so close because he had not expected to see a fishing boat and had misjudged the vessel's size.

Lighten their darkness

Our lights were obviously no help to us. Even when a ship is keeping watch I have doubts about the value of a yacht's legally required lights. This is not the Solent where yachts are commonplace. Out here, commercial skippers probably do not expect to see little masthead tricolours. That ship might have seen our masthead light and judged from its height that we were miles away. Why not? I've been surprised often enough, watching a tricolour and then suddenly finding how close the yacht is when I see its hull and sails. Deck lights are no better. They are too low to be seen half the time, and never by a ship keeping a sporadic watch.

From now we assumed that our safety at sea depended on our own lookout. A ship will not see any of our lights, so we might as well run with just a white paraffin light hung in the rigging and keep our batteries well charged for other things. Another yacht will see it if they are keeping watch.

A ship will only see us on radar, but I have little faith that they keep good radar watch either. Four hours after our encounter with this fishing boat, a small coaster crossed our bows close enough for Julia to alter course to pass round its stern. Half a mile away, in bright daylight, looking through the binoculars, I could see no sign of a turning radome on that well-maintained coaster.

Five days and 600 miles farther west, we saw our next ship. This was a large cargo vessel heading north-west to America. It was a dark night and we saw the glow of the ship's lights long before we could make them out. We put our tricolour on, for form's sake. As we crossed astern about 2 miles off, there was no sign that the ship was aware of us and no answer when I called them on the VHF.

There is a very big lesson here. Our log entries show that we saw more ships at night than during the day. This cannot be because more ships were out and about near us at night. It has to be due to our watch keeping and their visibility.

We did not keep formal watches during the day, but the small size of *Petronella* meant that someone was usually on deck. We do not look for ships by day because it is pretty certain that if something gets close we'll see it before we hit it. At night the main reason for being in the cockpit is to look out. We logged very few ships at all on the crossing, but all those we saw during the day came as a surprise. Two were only 3 miles away when we spotted them, and one of these was right on our nose where we could hardly miss it. A ship a few miles away is less distinct in day-light than their lights are at night.

Imagine, then, if after those first five days out of Africa we had concluded that there was no shipping around and that we did not need to keep night watches. Every day would confirm our view that there were no ships, and every night we would be oblivious to those that passed. With good luck we would arrive in the Caribbean well-rested and able to report that there was so little shipping that watches were not needed. And others like us would say the same. And with just a little less luck we would have had a very bad fright one night, or even been run down.

One for me, two for you

Once we got used to making passages of a week or more, there was a very simple way to assign our night watches. We decided that six hours off gave enough time for good sleep, so we set three-hour watches. If someone wanted to stay up longer, that was fine by the rest of us, but it wasn't essential to the scheme. In the waters of the south, a three-hour watch is no hardship. I have known the screaming desire to cut short an hour-long watch in the north.

As skipper, I was always on call and therefore spared the most tiring set of watches. After me, Magnus was second line of defence, to be called by Julia if she encountered crop circlers, aliens and such like during her watch. So he too got an easy night if one was going. Then, since not much was expected to be happening on most nights offshore, we could have the most novice-like of us up there for more of the time. By that fine logic, Julia was sacrificed to the god of sleep deprivation and usually stood two watches. If there was any chance of land coming up, we jiggled the watches to have Magnus or me around.

The final assignment of watches was designed around our sleeping habits. My habits are bad. I need a watch that starts well after dark and allows me to sleep in the early daylight, when I can feel that the crew are in control. Julia was also a light sleeper, but not so disturbed by boat noises as me. She could sleep during the day. The timing of the watches coincided with dusk. In the southern waters it gets dark quite early, so Julia started her first watch at 7 pm.

That was what we did. I think it worked well for us.

Running lights at sea, ha ha

A very different kind of close encounter with a fishing boat at night also illustrates the impotence of lights at sea. The fishing boat didn't have any. That's sometimes the local way of doing things.

We were two nights out from Dakar and running with all sail up in a steady force 3, sailing hard to make the Casamance river by Christmas Eve. The night was pitch-black. The large fishing pirogues[1] with crews of ten or fifteen men work all night without showing proper lights. The trick is to flash your own lights every so often

---

[1] A dug-out canoe in form, but usually built from planks. Varying in size from 10 feet to 40 feet and with crews of from two to twenty men. Powered by outboards. Quick, but I wouldn't call them seaworthy.

and then look to see what lights come up in reply. The trick can't work if you have your lights on all the time. The point is to make the other boats out there show themselves to you, not for you to be in permanent view of them.

> Sod the gybe. No time to handle that or to fiddle with the preventers. I bore off hard and *Petronella* came round, the sails tried to come over but couldn't, our speed barely dropped, and we flashed past the pirogue with its stern 25 feet away. I was swearing at them and they, no doubt, at me. There was certainly a lot of yelling. I shoved the tiller down and came back on a course that did not have all the sails backed, and tried to calm myself.
>
> I didn't like running without lights, but that hadn't been the problem. Finding a pirogue offshore that didn't even have a torch to shine at us was the problem. How many more of them might there be?

I was alone on watch. I flashed our masthead tricolour on. Up came three or four white torch lights from all around us. This was more than usual. Only one ahead of us was on anywhere near our course, so I bore off and that seemed to be that. Because they were rather near I put the tricolour back on. As I closed with the pirogue, they began to flash their light. I assumed they were making sure I knew where they were. I flashed my torch at them, just to show willing. Then I heard the shouts. I bore off a bit more. Clearly something was not right, but we were missing that pirogue by a long way. There were more shouts in the dark night. Some were not coming from the vicinity of the torch. I bore off even more. *Petronella* was sailing by the lee, our preventers straining to hold the gybe. The pirogue's light now shone not at me, but somewhere ahead, and I made out another large pirogue in its beam. This was stopped in the water, almost dead ahead and very close, very lacking in freeboard with its nets all out, and with a very agitated crew. *Petronella* was coming down on them at 6 knots with her sails pinned in place with preventers.

We were all lucky that night. No wonder the crew in the pirogue were so agitated. Twelve ton *Petronella* making 6 knots with all sails flying must look like Juggernaut with a bow wave to a crew at water level, hauling nets. The pirogue was probably 30 feet long, ancient wood but heavy planking, and itself weighing several tons. With those nets out, *Petronella* would have ridden up its side like a ramp and probably holed herself while cutting them in two. The three of us, and 15 or so of them, would have been swimming around in the dark in 50 feet of water 6 miles off the coast of Africa.

Scope to improve

You should get good at raising your anchor, because you'll be doing a lot of it. You will need to know when you are dragging and, to save yourself a lot of unnecessary work, also when you are not. You will need to master anchoring fore-and-aft and to escape from small harbours leaving at least one of your anchors buoyed for collection later. Don't bother practising. You will learn as you go.

With only a manual anchor winch we always let the boat do most of the work of breaking out, but recovering the dangling anchor and chain is down to crew muscle. That was why we tried never to anchor in more than 30 feet of water. Even in 30 feet we usually laid 80–120 feet of chain. We dragged too often and I came to distrust our Bruce anchor on a short scope. Perhaps the Bruce did not suit the hard bottoms, but I think a CQR may be a better general-purpose anchor.[1] Holding improved when we got to *Senegal*, where the bottom was usually an excellent thick mud mixed with shells. Then our problem was breaking the anchor out of this vice.

We learnt our techniques for the stern anchor in the Canaries. In the much-to-recommend-it-compared-to-the-others harbour of Arguiniguin, yachts commonly use a stern anchor to hold their bows into the gentle northerly swell. When the north wind

Crew tactics conference on the bow.

strengthened and pushed a big swell into the harbour, we had to raise both anchors to clear out. The solution to what looked like an insoluble problem was easy once I could face leaving one of my precious anchors behind. We hung on our bow anchor, coiled as much of the stern warp as possible, tied a fender on it, pitched it overboard, nipped round the headland to the flat calm of Porto Cementos, and two days later returned to Arguiniguin to pick up our anchor in easy conditions. It is hard to do this when you have never left an anchor behind before. Believe me: do it.

Letting go

Long-distance yachts do a lot of anchoring, but not always well. If you are especially gifted, you will learn how to spot the best place to drop anchor in a harbour you have never entered before. I used to come straight into a place, spot a gap, and let

---

[1] Both Bruce and CQR are types of plough anchors I believe, but the CQR seems to dig in more readily and may be less inclined to lift out as the boat rides back and forth over it.

go. Lesson one is: that isn't the best technique. I am more circumspect now. I dither about, trying to guess why the best apparent spot is still vacant, what scope others have let out, and when the different hull shapes will start to swing. I motor alongside and ask other yachts what the bottom is like. Then I wonder if the row to shore is too far or if I want those jagged hard rocks as a lee shore. That is lesson two: inelegant but sure. I watch other yachts with admiration as they swoop into a strange harbour and let go in what, once they are settled, is clearly the best spot. That is lesson three: the master at work. At the moment I am on lesson two, and I do not give a damn how dithery I look as long as the anchor holds, we do not have to re-anchor after half an hour, and we have clear swinging room.

Kitbag

A journey of self-reliance like this brings its own standards by which to judge equipment. Choose gear that saves you time and increases crew safety when doing exposed tasks. Prefer kit that is easy to understand and easy to maintain. Standard parts are easier to get hold of, especially when you have crossed to a new continent.

I praise unstintingly the GPS and solar panel, the lazyjacks and boom gallows, galley foot pump, salt water tap and safety belt, the life-saving Megabeam and simple canvas cockpit cover, but some lesser items added a quantum improvement to the quality of our life.

A digital voltmeter made me independent of others when sorting out electrical faults, and brought great peace of mind. An electric screwdriver turned screws in the most awkward of places, out of sight and barely within reach. A rechargeable drill made the many holes that occupy my days and a little vacuum cleaner sucked up the dust. A dry-cell battery charger allowed torches, clocks and radios to work, however long we were at sea. An inverter meant having the more reliable 240 volt versions of electrical equipment instead of the 12 volt.

Choose quality. Maglite torches are expensive, but they work when you need them. Rubber-bodied snap shackles on beckets cost silly money but are worth it, in reducing time on the foredeck wrestling with lines under load. I held my nerve in the shop and bought four. If you don't think four is the right number, buy five rather than three.

Innovate rather than buy expensive chandlery. Our shower was a 1 litre garden spray, used on deck. Our canvas bucket was an ex-army horse-bag. It hauled water, held tools, was an overnight larder for flying fish, and a drinks cooler employing the evaporation principle much favoured on *Petronella*.

Forget aesthetics. Shock-cord was invented for me: sail ties; holding dinner plates quiet; stopping bottles rolling; keeping the table top from banging; keeping genoa sheet blocks upright; holding locker lids open.

New aerial routes

The future belongs to Information Technology. Here is what my experiences make me look forward to.

Radar

It was never needed on this journey, but I would have it if new developments brought the huge price cuts and increased functionality that made GPS a small-boat standard. Radar has tottered on the technological brink for nearly a decade now without changing its essential nature. When will we see a miniaturised radome that looks like no radome at all, and a flat screen that also plays videos?

Portable VHF

I would like one to allow communications when away from the yacht. I put less weight on its role in the liferaft after abandoning ship unless the search has already been triggered.

Short wave radio (SSB)

I longed for one of these to hear about friends, weather, navigation, places to visit, and places to avoid.

Satellite telephone

This, surely, is the real communications future, with huge development waiting to be driven by mass markets on land, able to revolutionise the things we take for granted or didn't even know could be part of life offshore.

If the future is electronic, what provides the power? The solar panel on *Petronella* changed my life but, like radar, this technology has teetered on the brink of a break-through without delivering. Even if a breakthrough comes soon, solar panels may lose out to a radically new technology, such as fuel cells, if this can give us greater control, certainty and capacity to power-up larger banks of batteries, and from there even to re-engine our boats.

Sails

♦ *Sails need to survive the full range of weather conditions – storms, but also calms.*

♦ *No sailing rig is ideal, but almost all will get you over the ocean. Tweak and tweak again. Aim at simplicity and flexibility, safety and robustness.*

♦ *The cutter rig was right for us. The staysail got more use and abuse than any other working sail.*

♦ *It's always a compromise of what is ideal and what it costs.*

♦ *Hi-tech gear can give severe, awkward and wholly unexpected problems when it goes wrong. We learnt some simple lessons in managing foresail roller reefing. I wouldn't do without it.*

♦ *Mainsail reefing must be quick, safe, simple and well-tested – and ideally done without coming head-to-wind. There are wonderfully cheap and effective ways to control the main before you resort to hi-cost hi-tech.*

♦ *Evolve the new sails needed for this route from what you know.*

♦ *Make sure your trade wind rig works while you still have time to change it.*

Two of everything, three of some

The mysteries of the sea for me include tides and the workings of a diesel engine, but the greatest mystery of all is the sails. I've read some truly informative books that give simple and comprehensive explanations of how sails convert wind into forces that drive the hull. It's all to do with vectors. Unfortunately, the moment I put these books down the clarity of the explanation dissolves. I try to explain sails to others but my eyes glaze over, my mind turns to treacle, and the best I can say is: 'Mankind has sailed the seas for thousands of years and it's only in the last five or six decades that we've discovered the aerodynamics of how sails work. It's all to do with vectors.' Well, our ancestors got to places by ignorantly pulling bits of string, and so did I. When the choice is to spend time on practical matters or analyse theoretical arguments, then go out there and just do it.

The sails you carry on an ocean crossing make rather an important contribution to that central question of whether or not you will survive. My working rig of jib, staysail and main is fine from force 3 to force 6, but this leaves out quite a bit of what I thought might meet us. I worried about how the rig and sails would stand up to storms and near-survival conditions. What if a sail blew out? Some of my sails were well over ten years old, but still seemed to have a lot of life in them. Anyway, for lack of house-room they were coming with me, and would be used every day on the ocean. To reduce the fear of a blow-out, I carried two of everything – and three of some – and the poor little boat was full of sails.

Big wind is a big worry, but it isn't the only one. I worried about calms and light winds too. Your first passage of a week or more will make you realise how vital light weather sails are. *Petronella* is too heavy to be driven by her working sails when the wind is light. Then, on top of storms and calms was the concern specific to this great adventure: the trades, and the sails needed to run downwind for weeks on end.

The sail wardrobe on *Petronella* has developed with all the rationality of Topsy. *Petronella* came with a full set of working and storm sails, and I doubled this number by buying replacements before they were needed. Then I added a sail or two left over from other boats, which didn't fit but might be useful in a crisis. Then I thought about new light weather sails. The cruising chute only did part of the job so I added a multi-purpose headsail as well, with the new sheets, halyards, uphauls and downhauls that go with it. Then I bought spare lines, of course. It's a tight squeeze in the forepeak now.

I already liked the theory of the cutter rig for shorthanded, long distance sailing so I was lucky when *Petronella* came with cutter rigged. And that is probably what most boats on this ocean adventure have: the rig they were built with. In which case, learn to love your rig and make it better at the things you want from it. Sure, some rigs are better suited to blue water sailing than others, but in practice almost every rig ever seen on the coasts of Europe has crossed the ocean. Having the wrong rig on your boat is the lamest excuse for backing out of this project.

You must work continuously to make your rig more secure and safe. In the years before I cast off from England I had made many changes to the rigging, the sails, and how I used them. Even then, I wasn't finished. We improved the gear after crossing Biscay and again by the time we left Africa. And then we learnt what was really needed for a month of running down the trades, and all about downwind sail balance and reefing.

Roll up, roll up

The lighter the crew and the more singlehanding to be done, the greater the benefits from headsail roller reefing. I hope never to go back to the wet days of changing sails at the end of the bowsprit. Roller reefing does the vital job of keeping me and my crew off the foredeck in heavy weather.

> I yelled, 'Here's a big one!' We were diving into a wall of water twice as tall as Julia who, on the end of the bowsprit, was suddenly being squashed by a huge wave.
>
> Julia was up there for fun . . . If she had been there for real, crouched on the narrow bowsprit, jamming herself against the stay for support, head down like a bull's eye target for every rogue wave, trying to keep one hand free to work, suffering weightlessness as the bow rises and falls through 30 feet, then I would not have thought her soaking was such a joke.

The constant debate on sail handling and rigs is about hi-tech versus low-tech, complicated versus simple, mendable-under-way or not. Sometimes this translates into an argument about expensive versus cheap, but for most of the time these are two different arguments. Headsail roller reefing is the thin edge of the hi-tech sail-handling wedge, and the lesson we learnt on our trip comes down to this: no matter how robust the gear, the more hi-tech it is, the more you suffer when a little thing goes wrong. This doesn't invalidate my preference for the gear, any more than the occasional hangover invalidates my preference for red wine over water. Abuse is something we should pay more attention to.

Julia demonstrated a head for heights, considerable upper body strength, stoicism in the face of a battering, and nearly as much grace as an Olympic gymnast. When she returned to deck, the genoa slid up the track as smoothly as silk.

Old-fashioned sails are not without their drawbacks, of course. We also learnt some lessons about the other sails too: there are many simple pieces of gear to tame the mainsail; you should have these even if you don't have the more expensive reefing and control systems; you will do more mainsail reefing than you could possibly realise; the gentle trade winds will blow hard at times and try to trip you up; our old-fashioned, sometimes vicious, boomed-staysail was the true hero of our rig.

Main work

Mainsail reefing is a completely different kettle of fears. No other sail carries the sheer brute weight of the mainsail and its boom. Reefing means taming this just when the weather conditions are set to go crazy. A Bermudan-rigged boat must always come onto the wind sufficiently to allow the mainsail to flap freely. On most traditional rigs this means the boom and lines are also flapping freely, and reefing involves arm wrestling them into submission. The same is no doubt true of hi-tech rigs when they go wrong, although I have read with longing of mainsail reefing systems that allow old men to win transatlantic races without having to take their slippers off. I would settle for less. I would settle for mainsail reefing that reduces the time I spend hanging onto the end of the boom with only one foot on deck. The friends who see me performing this little trick on dark nights with a heavy swell running, which are the conditions when most reefs are put in or shaken out, agree.

I woke in near-panic. Last night, putting in a reef, I was leaning right off the quarter with all my weight on the boom . . . both hands unravelling a kink in a reefing line. We were a 1000 miles offshore . . . running at 6 knots.

Unfortunately, bank managers have affected my sailing decisions and, as a result, I have gone for an incremental rather than radical investment. I have gradually changed the controlling equipment on the periphery of the mainsail. This has been wonderfully cost-effective. The improvements in personal security and sail control are huge relative to the cost of new kit. Even so, there is a limit to what can be achieved. But however I improve my slab reefing, it is still, at bottom, slab reefing.

Lots of little changes can be done: re-siting cheek blocks to make better angles for reefing lines; using thicker lines more comfortable to grip; adding a deeper reefing point. One of the bigger changes was to fit lazyjacks, and then the main was suddenly tamed. The great bag of sail usually left after the main was reefed was gone now. Life was easier and safer, whether singlehanding in a narrow river or dropping sail on a storm-tossed ocean. There is no reason not to fit lazyjacks to conventional mainsails. The design and fitting of the cheek blocks and lines is truly trivial.[1]

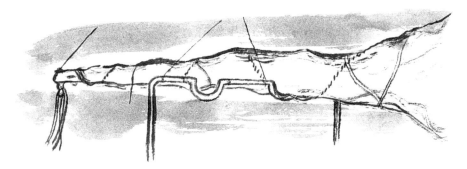

Strapping the boom in a steel gallows gives a greater safety factor.

A second major addition, made just before leaving England, was a boom gallows. A boom that swings even 6 inches when reefing is potentially dangerous and prolongs the job. Strapping the boom in a gallows makes for greater safety, but I had another benefit in mind. Of all the annoying noises a boat makes when rolling in a windless swell – the click-clack of plates, the thump-thump of binoculars in their rack – none matches the smack-crash of the tightly sheeted boom slamming over the few inches that cannot be removed, no matter how hard the sheet is cranked in.

Our simple gallows of bent stainless steel solved all of that and gave a strong handhold when going forward, a safer place to hang a storm light and, best of all, a place to fasten the front end of the little canvas awning that was to save us from the tropical sun. We even had a place to hang Magnus's aroma-rich Spanish salami. I cannot praise this simple bit of kit enough. The design and fitting was simplicity itself.

Even cheaper and easier to fit was the main boom preventer. I live in fear of the accidental gybe. I mean, think what it tells the watching world about my competence on the helm. This latest design is the culmination of many previous ones. It does away with searching in lockers for lines when it is urgent to have them; or of balancing on tiptoe to reeve through the end of a sheeted-out boom. I am surely

---

[1] I used John Campbell's design in *Easier Rigs for Safer Cruising*, and friends have copied it from me.

not alone among sailors in finding so many operations that involve leaning precariously over the side of the boat while trying to tie a knot with one hand.

One preventer line runs from the kicking strap plate on the boom to a point at the outer edge of the deckhouse level with the mast. Then round a block and back to a cleat within easy reach of the cockpit. A similar line runs on the other side of the deckhouse. These are permanently rigged and left slack until needed. Then the line is taken to a sheet winch and cranked in. Simplicity itself.[1] These lines do more than prevent a gybe. They help keep the crew on board when reefing or furling the main. They keep the boom in position when it is holding up an awning in port. I have even seen underwear hung out to dry on the lines, although I should tell you that this is not common. Best of all, they are effective gybe preventers, able to be engaged quickly, but also to be disengaged even quicker, without anyone leaving the cockpit.

Make damn sure that the preventer blocks and fittings are strong. We blew apart two 12mm blocks from carelessness during the trade wind crossing, when a single line cannot always hold a gybe. We learnt the tell-tale signs of a half-completed gybe. The block groaning audibly, the line stretching thinner before our very eyes. This usually gave our lightning reflexes enough time to push the tiller over or to uncleat the preventer. And then, of course, even if the gybe was unstoppable, the preventer saved us from tearing muscles and getting rope burns across our palms.

Drive out that calm

Petronella was heavy before we loaded the tons of ocean-crossing stores. Then her marks went under water and stayed there. In crossing trim, any boat that once ghosted happily in force 2 is wallowing in a force 3. Our working sails needed rein-forcements when the wind dropped to a force 3 or less. I ruled out a spinnaker. It doesn't fit my view that even a crew of three are just serial singlehanders when we stand watches. Anyway, *Petronella* does not have spinnaker gear.

Cruising chutes, invented at about the time I bought *Petronella*, seemed to be the answer so I bought a large one. It still confuses me. After seven seasons I'm more adept at getting the thing out of its bag and up the mast in its wonderfully slinky sausage, and usually I snuff it down without being lifted off the deck like a tiny child on the end of a very large kite. It's the sailing that is unpredictable. When it is good it is very good indeed and pulls the boat like no other sail on board, sometimes for hours on end with impeccable behaviour. But on bad days, when there seems no way of stopping the wind getting round the back and collapsing the sail, no amount of fiddling with lines and angles will make it work better. Frankly, more important than anything we can do is its own bloody-minded reluctance to join in our great adventure.

For these failings I bought what sailmakers inelegantly call a 'multi-purpose genoa', or MPG. This is our deck-sweeping, foot-wrapping, hold-even-a-half-

[1] A clever device with clutch and wheel can be bought to do this job – it works, but it costs 100 times more than my DIY kit.

breath-of-wind sail. It is hoisted on its non-twist luff line and then rolled and unrolled like any other furled foresail. It has never failed to go up and down, and saves me the roller-coaster, lift-off-the-deck behaviour of the chute.

The advantages of the MPG got it much more use than the chute.The chute had to be set on one side or other of the bow and forced us to sail on a reach instead of a run. The rudder could not counteract the turning force of the sail and the main was needed to give a semblance of balance. Because we could use the MPG with the jib and main, we spent less time wallowing without any drive while it went up and down. It could be left hanked on if we chose, instead of having to be bagged each time like the chute. It was also more familiar to us than the chute, being similar to our working sails. By the time we were setting off from Africa we knew the chute was not a trade wind sail. I still have less than a full inclination to mount a spinnaker.

A sail for all seasons

The true hero among our sails is that mighty midget the staysail. It stood up to storm and calms, neither of which are good for sails. It was also a great team player, helping us get more from the other sails. At 100 square feet, this is small enough to be very easily handled, even though it has to be worked from the foredeck. Sometimes this good-natured triangle of sailcloth can get carried away with enthusiasm. Its prettily painted white wooden boom is sometimes hard to avoid on the foredeck, and he was nicknamed Mr Whackit from my very first season. If your boat is a sloop, try making it into a cutter.

Hoist by hi-tech

The perennial debate between hi-tech rigs and traditional took on some fiercely practical forms out there on the ocean.

Shredding techniques at sea

In the fierce gusty weather that came ahead of the first gale in Biscay, when rolling and unrolling the genoa to keep our speed up, disaster was just a matter of bad timing. When a big squall came through with the genoa still half out and flapping with the sheet eased, the cloth split instantly along a seam. Now we had a serious problem. We could roll in the bottom two-thirds of the sail, but the top portion would only roll away to where the split began. To drop the sail we needed to unroll the whole lot.

This was a cleft stick dilemma. We couldn't just leave the sail up, but if we unrolled it that split would race right along the damaged seam long before we had dropped it on deck. The foredeck was also rather wild and wet by now, and I, for one, was a bit lethargic from the motion. The weather forecast wasn't bad, so I thought we should wait an hour or three for the inevitable lull in the wind. There was no doubt but that we'd have the damaged sail down by dark.

And sew on . . . We became very adept at mending seams and found it good therapy.

Two days later the gale blew itself out enough to get the genoa down. The sail was now a tattered flag. The unfurled top section had beaten an endless tattoo on the forestay, murdering my sleep. I lay awake worrying that I would have to buy a new foresail and that the continuous hammering would vibrate loose some masthead fitting and bring the mast down. These are the thoughts of a nervous skipper in his sleepless hours before dawn. Or, in my case, in his sleepless hours before dawn, after dawn and any other time when I should have been sleeping.

The first lesson is that a torn roller reefing sail cannot be rolled away. If you can get it down, get it down immediately. This is not without risk. In a full force 8 with an unfurled sail refusing to come down, we would have had to slit the cloth with a knife just to get rid of it. In those conditions, and if Sod's Law did not apply, we would get most sail away before the enormous flapping of useless cloth damaged the integrity of our rigging. Actually, we later discovered that even in relatively calm conditions it is not a trivial matter to haul down a split sail that the wind has played with. The loose cloth and the violent lashing of the sheets had together created some knots that are not in the books by Ashley or Brown. Nor, I can tell you, do these knots have polite names. Even after much jiggling of the halyard and sheets and tugging at the luff line and other sailorly things, Magnus still had to stand at full stretch on the pushpit rail to reach high enough to haul the torn sail down. This is not something I would encourage even my fearless crew to do in the rising seas of a gale.

The second lesson was prevention rather than cure. More care should have been taken in shielding the foresail before loosening the sheet, so that it did not flap in the strong wind. Our seam was torn in the blink of an eye. No one could have wound the jib in quickly enough. Nor could we have got a traditionally hanked jib down any more safely.

The genoa was our one working sail without a spare. Hence my paroxysms of worry. This was to be a main driving sail. We were very lucky that we were able to get it rebuilt in Bayona just before we left Spain.

> **Log entry: from Canaries to Africa**
> I called Magnus up and explained the tricky manoeuvre if we were not to blow another headsail. We ran the boat off the wind until the mainsail blanketed the jib . . . we rolled the jib away with barely a flutter. Textbook stuff. Magnus came back on the wind. I wish we had done the same in Biscay.

Hang about

Our hi-tech roller reefing gear failed just as we were leaving Bayona for Madeira. I had a fair idea why. One small reward for being an impoverished boatowner was that I could still remember how the kit had gone together one wet day in Essex. The sections of tube that slide over the forestay are held secure by countersunk grub screws. A grub screw had fallen out of the bottom-most section of tube and the section above just lifted as we tried to pull the sail through it. It was not difficult to fix. We had a spare grub screw and Magnus, who is 6 feet 2 inches, could reach the join by standing on the top rail of the pushpit. It was a calm anchorage and only took the big lad 15 minutes at full stretch.

The next failure was more of a problem. It led to us hanging Julia from the mast-head. We were up the Casamance river in Senegal making day-before preparations for the ocean crossing. We were switching from the working jib to the more powerful genoa, a change we had done a dozen times on this trip. The silky smooth ball-bearing swivel that stops the halyard wrapping tight around the forestay as the sail is hoisted was jamming as we tried to haul it up. This swivel is machined to fit perfectly round the aluminium tube. A grub screw near the top of the forestay had unwound a thousandth of an inch or two and the swivel could not slide past.

We rigged the bosun's chair and hauled Julia to the masthead. She lassoed the forestay and tied a bight of line around the stay and herself. When she reached the errant grub screw she clung to the stay with her legs so that with both hands she could half-remove the grub screw, coat some threads with Loctite, and screw it back in. Then we hauled her back to the masthead, she untied her line, and we lowered her to deck.

Oh, the drama those few words gloss over. For a start, Julia had never seen an Allen key before and I don't think she believed me about the Allen bolts up there. She humoured me and looked resigned to having to do the thing all over again with a screwdriver when I came to my senses. Julia's brave willingness to go up the mast began to evaporate as I explained the task to her. If Magnus had not quickly hoisted Julia clear of the deck, I think she might have got out of the chair.

The last straw for her was probably when I handed her the little Allen key and said pompously, 'For God's sake, don't drop this overboard. We have no chance of replacing it in Africa.' At the masthead the slight movement of the boat 'pendulumed' Julia's body from the moment she could no longer hang onto the mast and shrouds. As the boat rocked to the gentle swell, she was bruised and battered. There she was, swinging like a pendulum and feeling that the next four weeks of our life depended on her not dropping a very droppable sliver of steel whose purpose she doubted anyway.

Do the French have a sense of humour?
Three of our French acquaintances were rowing by as Julia came clear of the masthead and her body slammed hard into the rigging. 'See how the English treat their women,' one called. I raised my fingers in an instinctive acknowledgement of his wit.

Three points come out of this:
- Clever reefing systems can fail badly rather than safely and you will never foresee all their little ways. Over the last eight years I had worked out strategies for all the potential disasters I could foresee, but I never gave a thought to the consequences of a countersunk grub screw unwinding by a fraction of an inch.
- A system does not have to be hi-tech to fail. Michael Ritchie, singlehanding on his junk-rigged Jester, put back from an OSTAR because of frayed halyards and not being able to re-reeve them at sea.
- Don't let French *bon viveurs* see you doing repairs.

We rigged the bosun's chair and hauled Julia to the masthead . . .

. . . there she was swinging like a pendulum.

Trade in that rig

We were planning a whole new sailing experience in running down the trades and yet we did not test it seriously until it was too late to re-make it. Out first chance to try our gear came when we had a foretaste of downwind sailing as we ran with northerlies from Spain to the Atlantic islands. We never took it. On these journeys we lacked the gear to pole out, and so keep stable, a big headsail. Instead, we relied on the mainsail for most drive. The experience demonstrated very clearly the fundamental drawbacks of long days running under main: its clatter and wear when running in light airs; and having to come into wind to reef or drop it in strong weather. At times we dropped all sail, and drifted rather than suffer the agony of winds too light to keep the main boomed out. Of course, we didn't realise that light wind might be less of a problem in the true trades. Whatever, we decided against the main as a running sail and planned to rely on twin headsails for the crossing, balanced by the trysail if necessary.

Before leaving England we had hoisted and checked the trysail, but never actually tested it as a running sail. Nor did we give it a thorough trial on our way down to Africa. I mean, it took an hour of hard work to clear the main out the way and raise the try, then another hour to drop the try and re-rig the main. It never occurred to us that the try would not work as a running sail in its own right or as a stabiliser to the twins *when we really wanted it to*. We looked at the try in the wrong way. We saw it as a version of our continuing problem with the booming-out pole. We focused on whether we had the gear to rig it when we should have asked whether it worked with the other components while we still had time to cobble together a working solution.

The failure of the trysail to stabilise the twins was hugely important. It did not give us the stability our lives craved. But equally important was the failure of our intended twin headsails. Again, we travelled thousands of miles without testing them properly. Once we had wood-screws to fix the mast track for the pole, it took five minutes to realise the rig lacked power. We had enough sails to treble foresail power, but we did not have the necessary second pole or fittings. Had we discovered this earlier we could have taken advice from other boats and made up new bits of gear. I have since designed a twin headsail to be rolled away as a single furling sail. It might work. It would be worth taking the idea to a sailmaker. But this, like any other idea of twins, needed more poling-out gear than we were carrying.

Poling-out gear is not just a matter of a stick with a couple of end fittings. It is about simple and safe hoisting on a lively foredeck. By clipping the outer end of the pole onto the sheet rather than the clew we reduced the muscle strain and balance needed for the most awkward task involved but, even so, coping with a 15 foot pole taxed us to our limits. Julia could not rig the pole alone and I could barely manage it. Only Magnus could do it alone safely. Usually we had two on deck for this task. And this is with the most expensive gooseneck fitting in the world (well, that's how it felt when I bought it). Safe poling-out gear is about fully controlled

The parcel of reefed mainsail wasn't neat but, with a rapidly rising sea and wind, it was where I wanted it to be.

release from stowage to use and back again, the shortest and lightest pole you can get away with, and the best end fittings money can buy. We were lucky that our staysail came with a permanent boom that was simplicity itself to control. No wonder we preferred to use this as our running headsail.

We might always have used the mainsail in the trades. I can't say. Winging along on main and staysail almost certainly drove us faster than twins, although some of this is a matter of perception. By the time we reached the trades we were frustrated if the boat was not throwing up a bow wave and bustling along. Ten tons of boat on a waterline length of 28 feet needs the power of the main to achieve this impression, even if the speed difference between the bustle from the main and the serenity of the twins might be as little as 1 knot. Also, running under main was no problem for the self-steering. Indeed, once we realised that the steering would not gybe we confidently left the main up overnight. The problem was in the rolling. But our version of twin headsails rolled us even worse. We should have known more about fast and stable downwind sailing before we hit the trades. We could have experimented in the UK, but the best place would have been around Madeira and the Canaries, with gentler winds and more sense of urgency.

Reefing and unreefing: we lay waste our hours

Whatever rig for crossing the Atlantic, you need a good way of reefing your mainsail. Reefing and unreefing was something we did almost daily long before the crossing itself, and on bad days we might be doing it every few hours.

Boat and crew are most exposed when reefing. On a calm day reefing might take five minutes, but we didn't usually reef on calm days. The crew wouldn't let me. In the usual boisterous conditions, when it is already too late, reefing might take 20 to 30 minutes. On a dark night in heavy seas, and on my own, it might take an hour and leave me exhausted and silently screaming with frustration at those little tasks that took so long. And that is without the snarl-ups that have me running from mast to cockpit and back or clinging to the slippery boom, hanging over the guard rails, fiddling with some jammed line I can barely reach.

Halfway across the ocean I woke from a doze in sweaty panic. I had just recalled that on the previous evening, when Magnus and I were reefing for the night, the moment came when I was leaning about as far off the stern quarter as it was possible to get, all my weight on the boom and therefore the topping lift, and actually using both hands to unravel the kink in one of the reefing lines that was stopping me from tightening the leech. It was as dark as dark ever gets. We were a thousand or more miles offshore, the ocean was 3 miles deep, a biggish sea running, sailing broadish on the wind, and making 6 knots. There were two of us on deck. Magnus was concentrating on me and the tiller. I was concentrating on that damned line. Neither of us wore harnesses. Neither of us knew where the harnesses were.

Read that paragraph again slowly. If the word 'idiot' doesn't come to mind, then you should retire from the sea and get little old ladies to help you to cross busy roads because you are a danger to yourself. I had done this so many times before. What was unusual was for me to realise how vulnerable this very stupid reefing system made me.

Don't jump to the conclusion that you need such hi-tech solutions as in-mast and in-boom reefing before taking your boat on this adventure. Even when hi-tech doesn't go wrong in itself, it may cause knock-on problems for your boat. You may end up being more competent overall if you evolve from the gear and methods most familiar to you. Run reefing lines through the boom, so they do not foul, or run lines back to the cockpit to save time at the mast. Lazyjacks will reduce time on deck, reducing exposure to waves and sudden rolling. Traditional systems can be tweaked to get rid of the small nuisances that carry major consequences.

I met a gaff ketch that had changed to junk. This was major expense. New masts, rigging and sails. Removal of bowsprit. The purpose was twofold: to reduce the weight of work in sail handling for the singlehanded skipper; to be able to reef in all conditions quickly, safely and without coming into wind. The change was rather extreme for my taste, given that the boat was only two years old, but the skipper had achieved the two things I want most in mainsail handling without sacrificing simplicity. This solution may not be relevant to you and the timing of such costly change might be wrong. But you might take the incremental route and still not achieve your aim, whereas grasping the nettle of radical change might get you there.

Entertainment and events

♦ *I worried about pirates, but a little drip was the more life-threatening.*
♦ *Entertainment is straightforward. You have to like looking at the sea. There is wonderful wildlife to help you enjoy the world around you.*
♦ *Plan some treats and let others just happen. Take more Christmas puddings than the number you first thought of.*
♦ *Some people can catch fish, but not everyone.*

Nothing is as it seems

You can spend a lot of time worrying about big things that never happen. I wanted to know what events would threaten my health, limbs and life. I also wanted to know what wonderful events might happen as well, since even I can't sustain fear forever. Well, we had some good times, but it was a drip that came closest to sinking us.

Be they pirates?
Mauritania is the pirate coast and we were advised to keep at least 80 miles off. I added a bit. We kept at least 100 miles off, but usually nearer 120. The idea of pirates scares me. We can't outrun them and we can't outgun them. If we had Molotov cocktails, as I know one German yacht does, we might set ourselves on fire instead, and probably all because some innocent fisherman wants a cup of water.

We had a close-run thing one night off that worrying coast. Magnus wrote: 'Two ships came up from behind. Mauritanian pirates? Too scared to board us?' I'm grateful we got the scaredy ones. We never saw any others.

Flotsam
Nothing remains the same for long on the ocean. One morning between the Canaries and Africa, debris seemed concentrated into a tide-line, with us trapped there too for lack of wind. It added to the dreary nature of the overcast day. We were beginning to think the sea was dead, having seen so little ocean life since leaving the Canaries. Then four dolphins came and lazed around the boat for half an hour. A short while later three dorados swam with us as we blew along in a new breeze. These dorados were sleek, beautiful blue fish about 3 feet long, tails finished in gold. They swam at the bow like dolphins and rushed away after prey. This was the first time we saw dorados with us.

In the early afternoon a shark fin slowly cut the water and circled us. We never saw the shark beneath the fin. Soon after this we passed the biggest turtle we had ever seen. He was sitting so high in the water we thought he had borrowed an airbed. The turtle watched us with little black eyes as we drifted by, no more than 20 feet away, and we watched him. This was the first turtle we'd met that did not dive when we came close. Our dorados dashed off and swam right beneath the turtle, close enough to rub their fins on its belly. Now all day long we saw jellyfish and strange small creatures that occupied the surface and the water just below. We hadn't seen any of this when we'd been sailing hard on the previous days. Perhaps we had come into some ocean tide-line where life congregated. A day of slow progress made us part of the sea world.

Bad orcas

One mid-afternoon on a quiet day, off the coast of Africa and heading for Senegal, we heard the sound of a larger-than-usual dolphin breaking surface two boat-lengths off our stern. This was odd. We had seen no other dolphins and there were no dark streaks coming in towards our bows. We watched for it to rise again. What came up just a boat-length away was more massive than any dolphin we had seen. We had a very clear view as it lazily surfaced and then slipped under again. It had a distinctive pattern of black and white. I knew immediately this was a killer whale. An orca.

The orca resurfaced 50 yards away, heading south, and we sheeted to follow. Over to the south were two more orcas, probably 500 yards away. We failed to close the gap and the last we saw were the three creatures rising high in the water as humans might before taking a big breath of air. Then they almost stood on their heads, perhaps to dive deep.

This was our talking point for the rest of the day. When we reached Dakar we met a French boat that was attacked by killer whales right where we saw ours. Another French sailor in Dakar said a pod of orcas was always there and always looking for trouble. Bad orcas, but I was still glad to have seen them.

The deadly drip

Two days after we left Africa was a bad time to start sinking.

While in Senegal I connected a sea water galley tap to the engine inlet hose. It instantly transformed our standard of washing-up. We no longer had to lean over the side streaming a dirty pot in a strong grip. Life was safer on deck too, though less entertaining. We saw less of Magnus teetering on the stern with the canvas bucket when sea water was needed.

I was so very pleased with myself that I was not bothered by the small trickle of water on the floor by the new tap. I found the leak in the tap and fixed it. Still the water ran. I checked the engine inlet connection. It was fine. Still the water ran. I crawled into the engine compartment and saw a trickle running down the side of the hull. I traced the trickle to a nearby, but wholly inaccessible, through-hull fitting. This, the outlet for the bilge pumps, is normally above the waterline, but we were laden with stores, and had heeled over to port since Africa, regularly being slammed on that quarter by waves. Being normally above the waterline, and so hard to reach, I had never fitted the seacock specified by the surveyor in Plymouth.

I was not worried by so small a leak until I began to wonder why it should leak at all. We came through gales in Biscay with slamming seas and no water ran in. What had started it? Was it likely to get worse? We had four weeks and 2,500 miles to go on this tack, and if the fitting gave suddenly we'd be in a double bind. We would have water pouring in through a $1^1/2$ inch diameter hole and our main bilge pump would be useless since its outlet would be the inlet of the leak.

It was not physically easy to make a good assessment of the problem. The fitting sits high in the engine compartment, partially hidden by the fuel tank and timber frames. I am not enough of a contortionist to see and touch that fitting at the same time. I need a torch, a mirror and a spanner all in the same tiny space. My right arm has to reach over a beam to get to the fitting, and to manage this my head has to be facing downward and 12 inches below the fitting. Try this. It is not the easiest way of looking up.

This was a bad day to research the leak. First, we were making 7 knots on a beam reach in a bouncy sea. The boat made high-speed rolls and violent, unpredictable lurches. No job on board could be done easily. This would not be an easy job if the boat were knee deep in boudoir carpet. Second, I had lost to an African bug. Even standing up exhausted me. I had to force myself to overcome lassitude just to open the engine hatch. Having crawled into the engine compartment I had to lie still to recover. Looking at the fitting exhausted me. I had to rest before getting into position to feel for the leak. When the spanner fell under the engine bearer I rested before and after getting it out.

Julia squatted by the engine room, passing me tools. What an angel. If only she were in there and I was outside passing her the tools. Magnus rested. We all knew that he would have been asked to check the leak if there had been the slightest chance that his huge frame could have squeezed in. So he slept, guilt-free.

I diagnosed that the plastic piping had slipped from the hull fitting. The solution was obvious. Pull the plastic pipe free, clean it, smear it in lubricating detergent, warm the pipe till it becomes pliable and then whack the whole lot together. I've done this kind of job often enough. It wouldn't take ten minutes if access were easier. It might take as long as half an hour if the boat were ashore. In these conditions – absolutely impossible.[1]

The hose clip was not slack, but I tightened it and the others. This did not stop the leak. I crawled out of the engine room and lay on the galley floor, to worry in greater comfort. Could a wave slam into the hull just there and put enough

---

[1] I tackled this job in a boatyard in Trinidad. I spent two days getting the fitting off, and one day proving that I could not ever contort myself enough to re-fit it from the floor of the engine compartment. I cut a hole in the bulkhead behind the chart table and worked through that. This would have been disastrous enough at sea, since three days without a pipe on a submerged skin fitting would cause some water to enter the bilges. But much worse would have been the self-destruction of the plastic piping. I assumed, out in the ocean while working out what to do, that I would cut away the old pipe to remove the clips quickly and then use new pipe from the lovely spare length I carried. But the lovely new pipe had rotted after six months in the forepeak, and when I came to fit it in Trinidad the flexible plastic component split all along the harder insert of reinforcing plastic.

pressure on that fitting to burst it? We would have an instant unquenchable geyser and a doubtful ocean crossing. We were only a few hundred miles off Africa, but the nearest available land was on the other side of the ocean. If *Petronella* went down, our liferaft could only travel west with that wind and current. Two and a bit thousand miles is a long way to drift in a liferaft and I still hadn't provisioned a life-saving grab-bag for when we had to abandon ship.

I refused to over-dramatise the problem. I decided to look at it again when cured of the bug. In the meantime, I put two wooden bungs and a hammer by the engine hatch. I told the crew that if the boat started to flood they must get onto the other tack and whack the bungs into the hull fitting from the outside. Then they could wake me with a cup of steaming coffee and freshly made croissants lightly brushed with melted butter.

The empty sea and the sky

The real entertainment at sea is the sea, the sky and all things in them. If you get bored looking at the sea, then not even a shopload of videos will keep you entertained. I am fascinated by all the moods of the sea. Storms are just the most dramatic of the shows it puts on, with all the concentrated force of an orchestra hitting the loud end of Wagner. I also like the gentle times when the sea is a string quartet and the astonishing stillness of the calm, like the silence of a great cathedral when the rolling organ echo ends and before the coughing starts.

Looking at accounts of other people's ocean crossings I was surprised at how few sightings they made of dolphins and whales. Going down to Africa, and for the first half of the Atlantic crossing, we had dolphins alongside almost every night. Perhaps we were travelling at the right speed. *Petronella* is 2 or 3 knots slower than the typical 40–50 footers that make this passage. Dolphins can certainly stay with a boat making 8 or even 10 knots, but perhaps they don't see any reason to. Even with us they only stayed for a certain distance and then, as though they had reached the edge of their territory, would turn back or go off in a different direction. A fast boat will reach this territorial limit sooner, and the dolphins may

not see any advantage in swimming with it. More to the point, the fish the dolphins hunt may not be anywhere near these faster boats, but they may be travelling with us. Whatever, on the few occasions when we averaged 7 knots, we did not see dolphins.

You only see dolphins and whales if you look for them. We did not scan the waters, or anything like it, but we lived most of our life in the open and would always come on deck if we thought we could hear them.

The Biscay storms brought fun and excitement too

I was watching the dolphins. They were ranging alongside the weather hull, rising in the 10 foot waves like fast black shadows. I started to crawl along the deck to get a better view, but thought better of it. I was back in the cockpit, my hands gripping a cleat, and I didn't even see the monster wave. It just climbed up over the port bow until I looked up and there was no sky. Water came along the deck and hosed me across the cockpit floor. Water up to my neck tried to flush me overboard. The crew below playing cards heard a thud as my body hit the floor and asked what was happening, but they barely interrupted their game of cards. We had washboards in. I was wearing a harness.

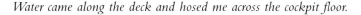

To begin with, we were excited by every dolphin. Later we became satiated. The ones we craved were the rarer, 15 footers and above, even though the smaller species were most fun, playing in our bow wave and turning over to watch us watching them. We tried to see how they signalled when they were going to take another dolphin's space, how they indicated annoyance, who was the boss. They swim in such a tight pack in the bow wave, and arrive at such high speed from behind to take pole position, that collisions seemed inevitable, yet we never saw them bump. Occasionally one would slap its tail in the face of another just as it rose to the surface. We wondered if this was a rebuke to a pushy colleague or even if the splash was meant for us. I wouldn't put it past them to let us know who is boss, them or

Water came along the deck and hosed me across the cockpit floor.

us. These are powerful creatures with immense skill in the water and what looks like a sense of purpose. So much of what they do looks to us like enjoyment. It's probably just to maintain a pecking order.

> **Log entry: between Madeira and Canaries**
> I wonder if the whales will reappear. Magnus says he heard whales two nights ago, but did not see them. Julia and I have no idea what a whale sounds like. Magnus does some blowing and whistling and eye rolling, which he says is exactly how a whale sounds and looks. We thought we saw some whales yesterday, but they might just have been slow and fat dolphins.

We saw fewer whales than dolphins. They didn't swim with us, so we couldn't observe them closely. Anyway, we were in two minds about meeting whales. I had read the usual accounts of what they could do to a small sailing yacht and I didn't want to be out at sea experiencing this. But when we got our first clear sighting of whales all fear was lost to the excitement of seeing them.

On all stages of the journey we had flying fish rising in front of the boat. Kamikaze flying fish were on deck most mornings, along with tiny squid. Some flying fish were less than an inch long, miniature but perfect. The 8 inch ones were eaten as soon as a mealtime came. Unfortunately the larger flying fish that came on board overnight often managed to flap back into the sea or got washed off. On quiet nights those of us off watch and awake would hear a thump on deck and then the patter of bare feet as the crew on watch ran forward to find the fish. We never seemed to get our just deserts. We rarely had enough bio-mass to make a meal for all three of us.

> **Log entry: day 10**
> Yesterday a dozen black 20 foot pilot whales kept station behind us for an hour, almost surfing down the 12 foot swells, keeping just below the surface. Today we met three 30 foot whales heading due south. Huge, slow and stately. Not in the least interested in us. Magnus caught the first glimpse of them. They were 50 yards behind us when they surfaced and we were leaving them at 6 knots. Without that lucky glance we would never have seen them passing.

We saw less wildlife after we left Africa. Visits from dolphins were becoming more of a treat. An unusual group came one day, a mix of 8 to 10 feet long bottlenosed dolphins, and some larger flat-nosed ones up to 18 feet long. This was the first time we had seen two types swim together. They came up into our bow wave, but did not play games. They checked us out and overtook. Then just after dusk that day the fun-lovers arrived, flashing like white ghosts through the phosphorescence. They were hunting and gave us the best dolphin display of our trip. One leapt 10 or more feet out the water, time and again, arching its back before splashing down violently. We thought it was trying to dislodge a sucker fish. Another Olympic qualifier leapt, rolled over and came down gracefully on its back.

For one frantic five minutes we had dolphins leaping everywhere, putting up flying fish in a frenzy of escape. I was hit, and for the first time realised the weight behind these missiles. Magnus had a near-miss from the biggest flying fish we ever saw. It rose 30 feet away and headed for us. It seemed to see its mistake and rose higher to clear the boom. Magnus, hearing my shout of warning, popped his head up almost into its flight path. He felt the breeze as the fish flashed past. A direct hit would have taken Magnus overboard. A more socially responsible person might have jumped a bit and headed the fish down into the cockpit for us.

We captured four good-sized flying fish that evening. Julia gutted them; scraped off the scales; removed head and tail and wings; and fried them in oil with pieces of garlic. Flying fish are delicious.

Julia and the flying fish were a nightly entertainment. Her night watches were punctuated by little screams and much stamping as a fish slapped her face or dropped into her lap. It seldom happened to Magnus or me. I thought of encouraging Julia to strap a bull's eye target to her chest and keep a bucket at her feet.

Sweet treats

Treats are essential to a good crossing. We planned some, others just happened as appropriate. Christmas was the obvious big event and we had presents to give one another and others to share around. We celebrated Christmas in the mouth of the Casamance with crackers, balloons, paper hats, sparkling wine and Christmas pudding.

Magnus and Julia had birthdays as we sailed and we celebrated with special meals. On Julia's birthday we also played charades, apparently a Californian tradition. Julia was the only one who knew the rules. Magnus questioned her about why she wasn't very good at getting the answers and we learnt more about her previous birthdays. By this time we were rudely disrespectful of Californian traditions, so Julia's birthday treat became that she could tell us about all her previous birthdays, going on as long as she liked, being as convoluted and imaginatively untruthful as she wished. It was a hell of a party, with the boat cross-reaching through the dark at a good 5 knots.

With temperatures soaring, we needed balloons and paper hats to convince us it was Christmas.

We made our own Christmas card.

Christmas pudding is a good treat at any time. I wished we had carried more. Golden syrup steamed pudding, our alternative, lacked the occasion of a true Christmas pud. We had golden syrup pudding to celebrate crossing 50° west on the trade wind route. It was a triple surprise. First, Magnus decided on it just a few days beforehand, as something to look forward to. Second, we did not cross the 50° west line on the day of the treat. At midnight we were still only 49° 58' west according to the GPS. If I had got the sextant out, I could have managed a couple of sights to put us well west of 50° and probably west of 60° too with a decent enough roll. Third, it was our last golden syrup pudding.

Gone fishing

For every ocean sailor who catches fish every day there are a hundred who drag a hook all the way and catch nothing. The moment was always going to come when Magnus would fish for our supper. He had been subtly letting us know this since the trip began. Julia fell for this and gave him a birthday present of ridiculous rubber octopuses, guaranteed to catch fish.

On the occasion of the three dorados, Magnus choose the most brightly coloured octopus and tied it to his line. Julia re-fixed it more securely. Magnus was not a competent knots person. We discussed tactics. He made it clear that he would not touch any fish he landed and, since we couldn't persuade him, Julia and I put on rubber gloves and took up a steel pipe and a hammer. We wanted a quick, humane fish death.

Magnus stood looking down at our wonderful dorado, then dropped the lure. One darted for it immediately. Magnus shrieked and yanked the lure so quickly that the fish never reached it. Julia and I, rubber-gloved and icy calm, abused him for his nerves and he aimed his horrible rubber octopus on the head of the nearest fish.

The fish took the lure and thrashed the water. Magnus thrashed the air and staggered back off balance. The fish took one second to break the line and escape. Now we watched it leaping and thrashing to get rid of the hook. The horrible rubber octopus was a very effective lure and the best one we had. We'd like it back and the dorado doesn't want it, but inter-species communication was poor. The dorado disappeared over the horizon and we were left with its two companions. Magnus retired to develop an alternative lure. Surely they would go for anything? For the next hour or so he dropped silver paper and coloured line onto the heads of these fish, but none of them came within 6 inches of taking the hook. The octopus guarantee was real.

Hoo are yoo?

During our drip drama, a beautiful little bird joined us. He, for too short a time, became a diversion and entertainment. His problems were more immediately life-threatening than ours. He was exhausted and wasted no time in going below. Julia named him Manga Dei. A friend later identified him as a hoopoe.

> **Log entry: day 3**
> A visit from the most beautiful little bird . . . a fine cockscomb . . . and a really long beak, ideal for delicately picking insects out of flower trumpets. He flew below as soon as he reached us and just fell asleep. Julia adopted him immediately. Manga Dei had a bright personality and was forgiven for his loose bowels. He seemed to know that his ticket on board was paid for by Julia. Fortunately, he spent more time defecating on her side of the saloon than mine.

It was clear to all four of us that Manga Dei needed nourishment. We searched the boat for grubs and the like, but couldn't find any. Manga Dei had to live off breadcrumbs and whatever Julia felt was appropriate. We had no idea what class of feeder he was. Poor Manga Dei might have hoped Julia had read more books on birds, or that he had landed on a liner with a library and kitchens. We did our best, letting him sleep late in the mornings and with whomsoever he pleased. He watched everything with the brightest black eyes and occasionally took some exercise. At first he was not very interested in the world on deck, but after a while he took a look outside. He seemed anxious that we were not taking him home to Africa. He had not heard how pleasant the Caribbean can be for little long-beaked birds and, to be honest, we didn't have the statistics to prove it to him at the time.

We were all concerned that he wasn't eating. I mean, there was a good wind blowing and little Manga Dei was going to fly against it. He would need more than a good rest. He would need all his navigation skills, since he had probably not made

Hoo are You — our passenger hops in for a quick position check.

this return trip before. On the second day with us he became quite decisive. He went on deck and made a few tests of the conditions. We tried to discourage him. After all, he hadn't made a *really* nasty mess down below, and he was a very pretty little thing. But the call of home was too great and he took off. We were not sure what happened next. He did not, I thought, make a lot of height and I had the impression that he came down into the water sooner than he might have wished. There wasn't much we could do. He had made his move and we wished him luck. We weren't able to go back to find where he might have landed on the sea.

Medicine

- *Be prepared for rare afflictions, but they probably won't happen. This is a healthy life – usually. A lot of health care for this journey is getting the jabs and stocking up on malaria pills, like any other traveller going to faraway places.*
- *There are hazards at sea, like cuts and wounds not healing. Take medicine to cope with these seagoing hazards.*
- *Change the medicine you take for your usual trivial complaints, so that it copes with the slightly more stubborn form they will take on at sea.*
- *Observe the crew's behaviour towards health. It can be a form of entertainment.*
- *Beware the bugs of countries en route. Departure from Africa may expose you more than leaving from the Canaries. Never drop your guard.*
- *Seasickness and sunstroke are always with you. The subtler forms may affect you all without you realising it.*

Where's the anaesthetic?

Hypochondriacs go sailing too. I'm certainly not one myself, even if I gave a lot of thought to what might happen to us (well, *me* actually) during our voyage. I usually got most worried while reading the account of some bloody and unanaesthetised self-surgery. I particularly wanted to avoid removing my own appendix during a violent storm because I knew I would have difficulty reading the instructions on the ex-army scalpel set or holding the shaving mirror to see where to make the incision. I wasn't looking forward to stitching the wound either. I spent much time in the bath pondering whether to have my appendix removed before I left England but, like lots of things I pondered, the important lost out to the urgent. Removal of a happy appendix took lower priority than fitting seacocks to all the holes in the hull. And that didn't happen either.

The yachting press is a good source of gory stories about people who have suffered agonies. Frankly, you are better off avoiding this tittle-tattle. It is very hard luck if it happens to you, and you probably won't suffer much less by being prepared. I am about to re-tell the sort of story that the faint-hearted are better off missing, so I suggest the sensitive reader averts his or her eyes for two paragraphs and picks up the narrative there.

That most unlikely sea hero, Tristan Jones, describes the gruesome time when his eye was knocked out of its socket by ice on his first singlehanded sail. He was on his way north to see what a winter trapped in the ice was like, so I don't suppose that having his eye knocked out was likely to bother him as much as it would me. He heard a noise like a bolt hitting the deck and rather unwisely looked up to see what it was. The masthead sheave or block, following hard on the heels of the missing bolt, smacked him straight in the eye and he would have gone sprawling overboard if his faithful dog had not got its teeth into the seat of his pants. Recovering from this indignity, Tristan went below and, without further help from the dog, realised his eye was dangling down around his chin on a nerve fibre. He pushed the whole caboodle back into its socket and, uncharacteristically, sailed to the nearest port for medical advice. It seems the doctor felt that Tristan had done as much as any man could and offered no further surgery. The eye had never been too wonderful, and whatever had been the lifelong problem now seemed to have been sorted out. His sight was improved. This, with hindsight, is one of the few parts of Mr Jones that worked better after one of his many disasters than before it.

The point to this story is to illustrate that nothing much prepares a sailor for an incident like this. The first reaction of most of us on hearing a noise like a bolt landing on deck is to look up at the masthead rather than grab the nearest full-face crash helmet. Another point is that the first aid box is your *second* line of defence. The *first* is a large dog. But if you take one with you, make sure it likes you as much as this one liked Tristan Jones, and keep the seat of your pants in good repair.

The serious point lurking in this lateral approach to health care on the ocean is that cause and cure has more to do with what is going on around you than with your pill box. We had remarkably few medical problems, for which I am grateful, but these few problems could have been better predicted if we had taken more direct thought over who we were and what we were setting out to do. I don't mean that we didn't think long and hard about potential troubles and the contents of the medical cabinet, because we did.

Be prepared

We had covered all the basic ground of what might trouble us, but we hadn't gone into the deeper details of where a simple little complaint can lead. It doesn't usually lead far, but it can go just a little beyond what you are prepared for. We all came on board with our own little list of susceptibilities, but did not always come equipped to deal with them in an offshore sort of way. We knew that a number of maladies, such as seasickness and sunstroke, would be out there waiting for us and we went prepared to meet them. But we did not give sufficient thought to the more subtle forms these things could take and how that would affect us. None of us were ever bothered by the really big things that might have struck us down and that we had probably taken care to deal with. I carried strong painkillers in case my damaged back flared up. Magnus walked for miles on feet that had been broken in a fall two years before. It was the little things that got to us. What we lacked before we set off were a few pointers to help make our preparations more effective.

Staying healthy is not just vital for safety, but also to have fun. Each person on the boat will have their own style of health care, with its own consequences. Understanding this aspect of your crew is as necessary as understanding the social relations on board if you are all to remain a happy and focused crew.

On *Petronella*, Magnus had the clearest approach to health and medicine. He was a browser. He liked to have a little complaint running all the time, but not the same one. Sometimes it was a wart, sometimes a sty, sometimes an ear problem. The only things he never complained about were the things that really bothered him. At times his feet were so painful he simply did not want to stand on them, but he did nothing about them and never complained.

Magnus was also a performer. What appealed to him was the theatre of illness. To search unlikely places for the tiny tube of ointment. The conversations this set in train. To unearth the ointment and discuss whether the long-past use-by date really mattered. To stand unsteadily in a gyrating boat and try to hit the eye or the ear or the wart with the tiny nozzle of the tiny tube.

Julia had the neat, efficient approach of a nurse. Stop messing about and take the medicine. She adopted this style in treating herself and itched to sort Magnus out. She was withering about his failure to put the top back on the cream he used on his sty. Words almost failed her when she saw that the tube had already passed out of its use-by date when it was first opened a year ago. She seemed to think the sty was mainly caused by his cure.

My stance was simple. I am cavalier about cuts and bruises, and usually only take precautions afterwards. Then, as the niggling pain sears through me, I go all limp and useless.

Perhaps we were wrong to make Magnus chief medical officer. He went on the one-day course with St John Ambulance. He got the certificate to prove it. We would have done better sending Julia, but it only became obvious later that if serious medical work was needed, Magnus' role would be to talk someone else through the gory bits and let them wield the scalpel.

Band aid – the ineluctable modality of motor dysfunction

The first trial of most sailing journeys is seasickness. Mine is, anyway, and it isn't something I look forward to. Magnus has never suffered seasickness and I don't think Julia ever felt queasy. Stugeron (a drug that works on the inner ear rather than sedating the stomach) saved me from being seasick in our first days of head winds and foul seas, but the effect of feeling dopey and behaving like a zombie may not have been worth the lack of seasickness. I still cannot bring myself to take another Stugeron. Fortunately, I have discovered Sea Bands and they seem to work for me. I wore them whenever we sailed and I now carry spares for everyone who sails with me.

Once under way, seasickness never seemed to be much of a problem. I think this was because we ignored the more complicated signs of motor dysfunction brought on by severe motion sickness. Well, we would wouldn't we? We weren't feeling well at the time. I don't know whether medicine would have helped, but a bit of sympathy might have done. And a bit of understanding that we are all likely to be affected in some ways, whether medical or social, when the motion of the boat is severe.

First aid – missing potions

We carried a complete medicine chest and had basic knowledge about how to use it, but the main things we needed were not in it.

Our list of ailments was not very long. Crossing Biscay, Magnus developed a sty, to which he was prone, and my cut finger went septic, as cuts do when they get continuously reopened by pulling on wet, dirty, salty lines. We did not have good medicine for either until we reached Spain. In Madeira, Julia had a fever or possibly a type of flu, but just took some superior American form of aspirin. We all had cuts, scrapes and blisters, especially on our feet, but these needed no more than antiseptic stuff and sticking plasters.

In Africa, Magnus caught a cold and needed to buy decongestants. He also had an ear problem, which exposed our lack of medicine for the ears. I then got something large and sharp in my eye, and we discovered that we had eye wash but no eye bath.

So our carefully researched, no-expense-spared medical kit lacked stuff for eye, nose, ear and throat. Whole hospitals have been set up to deal with less. Our kit also lacked anything for the other end. I do not suffer from piles and never found the right moment to ask the others whether they did either, but halfway across Biscay it suddenly occurred to me that some anti-haemorrhoid cream or suppositories would have been better than the painful alternative. As it happened, we never bought any or needed any. I merely state this here for the sake of completeness.

Worst aid – something we drank

The worst medical problem, in many ways, was the stomach bug Julia suffered shortly after we arrived in Africa, which hit Magnus and me as we left. I have no idea what this was or what medicine would have beaten it. We took aspirin. The real issue is prevention not cure. The main sides to this are: care in eating and drinking; choosing your departure points with health in mind; and possibly not going to Africa in the first place.

The illness was debilitating but not life-threatening. It worried us because of what might have caused it and not knowing where it would end. It only became a threat to the safety of the boat because of its timing. There is never a good time to be sick but this bug chose a stunningly bad time to lay me out (the same time as the deadly drip!).

Health isn't just about carrying aspirins and suppositories, useful though they may be. Health must become a state of mind when you are putting yourself out of reach of an ambulance for a month or so. We lived by the watchword: prevention is better than cure. It's a pity we didn't live by the deed a bit more than the watchword. That African bug was almost certainly something we drank, although it might just as easily have been something that we ate or breathed, that stung us or bit us.

As soon as we got to Africa we faithfully boiled water and sterilised vegetables, as all the health books insist. We might as well not have bothered. We no sooner got out into the country around the Casamance river than we innocently drank a couple of pints of water that even the locals looked askance at. The water came out of a restaurant tap, so we trusted it. We wouldn't have if we had known that the tap connected to an uncovered cistern holding water from the rainy season and was therefore now months old. If we were going to get one of those dreadful water-borne diseases it was probably right there and then, in the best restaurant of the friendly little village of Karabane.

It was at least a week before Julia was badly ill and I really can't say if it was due to contaminated water. By that time we had wandered around the countryside, walked through a crowd of

The skipper got his inspiration from a wet tea-towel.

10 million flies feasting on drying fish, hauled river-muddied chain and warps bare-handed. We had drunk country palm wine from the bottle when it would have been prudent but churlish to refuse, ate cheaply in Senegalese restaurants rather than French ones, and spent a day at a local naming-day feast. We had showered in water from an open tank and anchored off what smelt like the main sewer of Ziguinchor, through which we also landed our dingy to get ashore. We must have been exposed to many more sources of sickness than that dreadful water at Karabane. Whatever, we all gradually went down with a sort of flu that took a week to clear.

The point about Africa was that we did not choose to live in a sanitised plastic bag. We took care to be hygienic, but of course we breathed the dust of Africa, even when still hundreds of miles offshore; we were in crowds where people sneezed, coughed and spat; a place where the drains looked foul, and the smell of putrid cat or donkey was never far away. The African air probably harboured a lot of bugs.

Julia had recovered from the bug on the day we left Africa, but Magnus and I now had her symptoms. Magnus was ahead of me. He was much better by day three at sea. I did not start to improve until day five. Had I been singlehanding, or had we all suffered at the same time, the sickness would have made all the normal activities of sailing hard, if not dangerous.

Thirst aid – more than a headache

Perhaps we were lucky or had taken more natural precautions against sunburn and sunstroke than we realised. We didn't suffer from these problems, despite having no cockpit awning, until we sailed well into the trade-wind belt. We used creams to protect our skin, and wore clothes as protection too, but we mainly wore headgear to protect from the cold and wet. Then, after four months of acclimatising, Magnus over-exposed for a few minutes and went down with sunstroke in the most amazingly short time.

The symptoms came on him in about three minutes. His body just stopped coping and we had to half-carry him below. He was overheated, dehydrated and out of action for a whole day. The solution was simple. We rigged a square of canvas over the cockpit and never had this problem again.

I wonder whether sunstroke, like seasickness, can have less obvious signs and may have affected the way we coped with things, and therefore also with the people around us.

Pre-aid – shots in the arm

Staying healthy is vital to the safety of the ship. It isn't just the sickness itself that you have to take into account here, but the timing of it in relation to the other things you must cope with when sailing.

We were very lucky, but I think most crews are. It's a healthy life on the ocean and most of the care you need is obvious and routine. We never had to resort to surgery or anything invasive. (Or, at least, I didn't. The crew sometimes had me worried.) We had more jabs than I care to remember before we left the UK, but these were all listed by our doctors and did not involve us in anything more taxing that rolling up a shirt sleeve. We took vitamins and other pills on and off to supplement our diet. No one lost teeth or hair, except to age, scissors and the razor. The single main medicine we took were anti-malaria tablets, which we bought in the UK but topped up in the Canaries. Again, the doctors provided all the help we needed. All we had to do was take the medicine, foul though it was and with a complicated timetable.

Without trying very hard, we got it just about right. But if we had been a little more well-informed at the outset, we would have coped that vital bit better.

Places

- *There are good places off the beaten track.*
- *Always be wary of wind shifts when in harbours in the Canaries.*
- *Go to Africa. It was the real adventure of our crossing.*
- *Trinidad & Tobago makes sense as your Caribbean landfall if you plan to go north and home again. Also, even if you don't. Of course it isn't Paradise, but it's damn close.*

Charts and pilot books only tell part of what I want to know about a new harbour. I dread harbours as places where other boats wait, like targets, to be hit. I want to know if there is room to stop and turn. Our two rules when entering any harbour were: appease the gods of chaos by getting ropes and fenders out; get your panic in early. A journey through 100 new ports was not an anticipated pleasure, but I gained a veneer of serenity. Having crew to shout at helped enormously. Really though, we never had much to worry about.

Pilot books seldom told me how well places would provide for our needs. We needed so much, being always in a state of preparation.

These are my idiosyncratic views on the standard Milk Run stopovers and the much more wonderful places off the beaten track which, with encouragement, you might well visit.

Spain

Gijon

This typified the north-west coast of Spain for us. It was barely mentioned in our two-year-old pilot. Yacht havens have sprung up quicker than a pilot book author can blink. Some, like Gijon, are in splendid old harbours. Others are little rafts of pontoons in *rías*, ideally placed for a night stop. Most were nearly empty when we arrived, and the people looking after them were as pleased to see us as we were to see them. South of La Coruña we came to assume there would be facilities for us wherever we wanted to go. I mean, the pontoon builders could spot a good anchorage better than we could. The Spanish *rías* have a yachting infrastructure to make the Solent envious.

Huge black clouds filled the sky, spray came over the 20 foot-high sea wall behind us, and we lay snug on the pontoon. Gijon has excellent local hardware shops. We explored them thoroughly during our three-day stay.

Bayona

You will almost certainly come here. Bayona is one of the main gathering points as boats head south. I never took to the place.

Aspects of Bayona were very attractive. We met old acquaintances and made new friends in the large outer anchorage. We found fascinating chandleries and a good sailmaker. We refilled our Calor propane bottles at the gasworks.[1] But the yacht club was unhelpful towards boats at anchor.

This is a racing club with all the flags and blazers and polished cannons to be expected. Club facilities are only available to boats on the club pontoons. This was frustrating especially as there was no room left on the pontoons and no public facilities in the town. Club rules forbade us to pay for showers, so we had to sneak in for free when no one was looking. This isn't as dishonest as it sounds. The club charged us to anchor in the bay. This angered all the anchored boats. No other Spanish harbour had charged for anchoring. To be fair, the club boatmen only came out occasionally to collect the dues, and if they thought there was no one on board they didn't knock. Ironically, this just made the whole thing worse. It was as though Fate conspired against those being asked to pay. Given how much Fate seems to rule the lives of small boats, sailors never like to think She has a downer on them.

Madeira and Porto Santo

Two pieces of advice for boats stopping in Madeira. First, spend most of your time in the neighbouring island of Porto Santo. Second, when in Madeira make sure you walk in the mountains.

Porto Santo could be on a different planet from Madeira. It is dry, its mountain peaks and steep-sided valleys being too low to bring the huge rains of Madeira. Its small population and tiny main town are more relaxing than Madeira but, above all, it has a secure anchorage and large harbour.

The southern coast of Porto Santo is protected from west through to east. There is good holding along a beautiful golden beach and you can see if the anchor has hit sand at 30 feet. A southerly swell is uncomfortable, but we always knew when the weather would get too bad for anchoring off the beach.

The harbourmaster came to invite us into the harbour. This harbour is a miracle of European Union generosity, being much larger than required for local craft. Good pontoons for landing. Buoys on concrete sinkers.

Porto Santo has limited equipment and services for yachts, but the important point is that it has some. There was stainless steel welding, a crane that could lift a 20 ton yacht, and hard standing within view of the port police.

Funchal, the main town of Madeira, was not a good anchorage and its marina was full that month with yachts rafted four deep. On calm days we saw boats dragging, after days anchored on the same spot. On one windy day half a dozen yachts dragged before re-anchoring deeper into the harbour. The best anchorage is up by the marina entrance, sheltered by the long southern breakwater, but yachts are

---

[1] We have always been able to fill British Calor bottles at local gasworks. Find them in Yellow Pages or the tourist office.

We walked between the twin highest peaks of Madeira on a brilliantly clear day.

forbidden in case they obstruct the cruise ships. Most yachts anchor there until the harbour officials ask them to move.

Funchal is a good place to get things done. It lacked good yacht chandlery, but we found metal stockists, welders, workshops, paint supplies and gas stockists in the older part of the town.

We walked between the two highest peaks of Madeira on a brilliantly clear day, using paths and stairways cut and fenced by some far-sighted earlier generation. In places the metre-wide path was the mountain ridge. In other places it ran just below the cliffy peak at the end of a valley. In other places it tunnelled through a peak of hard rock. This is volcanic country with needle-sharp peaks and steep-sided cliffs.

The Salvagens

The Salvagens are tiny uninhabited islands on the way to the Canaries. We obtained official permission to visit them in Madeira, to add spice to our journey south.

Log entry: fourth night from Madeira

We did not land at the Salvagens. We came slowly on them in a falling wind and worked through the rocky channel to the best landing place. The entry recommended in the pilot looked more difficult than our route. As we came up on the anchorage, so did the new onshore wind. We came inside the rocky approach to the anchorage, but the wind drove waves at the landing place.

Two wardens watched us from the rocky hillside, but made no move to guide us in. Perhaps they thought it too dangerous. Perhaps they were not ready for outside company. They didn't even wave back. The wind was good for the Canaries, so we hauled round and romped away.

121

The Canaries

Atlantic-crossers go to the Canaries because they're there. If they weren't, all you'd miss would be a handy cash-and-carry in the ocean.

Like most of the visiting boats we met, I was too uneasy about the anchorages to enjoy the Canaries. Foreign boats do spend years there, of course, and for them the information on the VHF radio net and some really heavy concrete mooring blocks make the islands a secure place, but cruising yachts never have enough local knowledge and they want to leave boats on anchor while they visit places ashore.

Los Gigantes, Tenerife

Los Gigantes is tourist apartments around a huge marina excavated from magnificent volcanic cliffs. It's called Los Gigantes because of these cliffs. It could have been named after the swell that comes round the harbour wall.

We arrived in a flat calm, but the swell from yesterday's southerly wind still reflected off the cliffs and into the marina despite the dog-leg entrance. We could only stay for one night, not the two we asked for. No room. This was what lots of boats found in this marina. No room. No want you.

San Marcos, Tenerife

San Marcos on the north coast looks like a mini Biarritz. The town opens up once you enter the pretty bay. We anchored within 300 yards of the town in 30 feet of clear water. Landing is on the beach or the slipway. Local fishermen told us that the south wind would soon switch to strong north-westerlies, and the placid anchorage would become a cauldron of white water, the entrance a wall of high breakers. We left.

Santa Cruz, Tenerife

We struck lucky in Santa Cruz, the island capital. By the commercial docks we saw masts of sailing yachts where no marina was marked. Mindful of the age of our pilot book, we rounded the main breakwater, motored up to a grand old commercial basin, and tied up alongside the wall. No facilities, no showers, not yet a marina, but only £4 a night, free electricity, good company and five minutes to the city centre.

I like old commercial harbours. They have usually ironed out their problems. True, a south wind straight up the entrance channel would cause a bad chop, but we would get out if that happened.

Yachts alongside us were painting and varnishing. A charter yacht from Scotland was starting major refurbishment. The costs were a fraction of British prices and the reliable weather meant they could programme tasks better. We did some work ourselves, found out more about West Africa, and copied charts for Senegal. The company you keep shapes what you end up doing.

Pasito Blanco, Gran Canaria

A relaxed but barren marina off the bus route. The restaurant shut at 6 pm. The tourist apartments are like a citadel. They repel the inquisitive.

Water available on the pontoons. Showers. Not a welcoming landfall.

Puerto Mogan, Gran Canaria

Marina Magnificent! It was large, well laid out, well maintained, and full of beautiful foreign yachts. People speak well of Mogan, but it was too expensive for us.

Arguiniguin and Porto Cementos, Gran Canaria

Don't be put off Arguiniguin by the huge concrete plant next door at Porto Cementos. You will need them both as winds shift from north to south.

Arguiniguin is not quaint and beautiful. It is real. A small fishing fleet uses the inner harbour and yachts anchor in the outer bay, in sand and protected by the large harbour wall. Long-stay yachts run stern lines to the breakwater between inner and outer harbours, their bows on heavy mooring weights. Close to the north shore is a sandy-looking plate of rock. To anchor there is to drag.

Most sailors remembered Arguiniguin with affection. Had I known about the cash-and-carry and Spar supermarket I would have bought less in Plymouth. A 'hole in the wall' takes Visa. Hardware shops in town. Diesel from the garage.

Porto Cementos is a wide sandy bay and pleasant village. Holding is good. Landing on the beach is easy. Good swimming. Without the cement works, this would be a popular tourist spot.

There are few shops at Porto Cementos, but Arguiniguin is seven minutes' walk by the short-cut.

Las Palmas, Gran Canaria

We went from Arguiniguin to Las Palmas by bus. Much better than going by boat. The main town of the island is not pretty, but has good chandlers, hardware shops and services. The photocopy shop on Emile Zola Street charged £1.50 for full-sized charts, done while we waited. If that shop is not still there, there will be others.[1]

Leaving Gran Canaria

National holidays and provisioning delayed us, but by Thursday afternoon we were stocked apart from water. We could find none in Arguiniguin. We needed full tanks. Canarian water was to be the basis for our Atlantic crossing. We only needed 20 to 30 gallons. Not enough to call a tanker. Not enough to justify a stopover in a marina. Anyway, we had spent our last peseta. I am not in the least superstitious, but I had no wish to start this next passage on a Friday. Not with my doubts about Africa and all. We would leave by midnight or not till Saturday.

We figured out which marinas had both water on tap and early closing. When the sun went down we went visiting. It was dark and the marina office deserted. We took no more water than they would have run off the next day. We were out while it was still Thursday. The crew knew nothing of my superstition.

---

[1] There is also a copy shop in Santa Cruz, Tenerife, which would be the envy of many London ones.

Africa – off the chart

Africa couldn't wait for us to arrive. It met us 70 miles away with a fine red dust that clung to our mast, rigging and sails after a sensational red dawn on our penultimate day. Our leaving experiences were not so different. Red dust covered us 800 miles offshore in the trades, and a million tiny spiders arrived one night 1200 miles out in the ocean.

Pilotage
Coming into Dakar is straightforward and easy in daylight. I would not like to attempt it at night. The local pirogues fish all round the coast day and night, and don't show lights until you are almost on them. A large pirogue of 10 to 20 men with its nets out is in no position to get out of your way. It has little freeboard, the underwater shape of a skimming disk, and the seagoing qualities of a saucer. When hauling nets the crew's weight presses one gunwale almost underwater and the crew performs a delicate balancing act. This was the first time we had seen pirogues. We jinked around several as we sailed around Goree and up towards Dakar. They were easy to see, crowded with men in yellow oilskins, but we later discovered that on a dark night an unlit pirogue is little more than a deep slash of black against the less deep black background of the sea.

Dakar, the capital of Senegal, sits at the southern end of a low promontory. Our first sight, when we were only 12 miles off, was the old lighthouse on a hill at the northern end of this. Then airport buildings and tall city blocks broke through the heat haze and the dust. At 5 miles off we could see a large wreck at one end of the promontory, and the island of Madeleine at the other end. We came inside Madeleine and then outside Goree island. We had been well offshore for over a week, but here we were again sneaking along a coast and heading for shallow water and traffic.

For this huge coast, with potentially some of our most difficult navigation and pilotage, we had the least information. We had no pilot books. Our charts were photocopies, out of date and collected haphazardly on the way. We began collecting this library at Madeira. We borrowed material from a New Zealand yacht, Swiss charts via an Irish yacht, typed notes from Americans, a sketch map from a French sailor, and pages from the *Rough Guide to Senegal*. All were out of date but invaluable. Everything we needed for this unplanned excursion came unstintingly from the community of yachts heading south.

Africa was exciting beyond any other landfall. In my case, exciting and foreboding. As a naturally timid sailor I had plenty of reasons other than practical navigation to bother me. Apart from being talked out of going to neighbouring Gambia by Foreign Office reports of a shooting war, I knew I would not have come this way without great confidence in the crew. On the last few days of our journey I subtly probed them to see if they were as anxious about the world ahead as I was. Their lack of even a single care about the Dark Continent was clearly the gross naïveté of youthful ignorance.

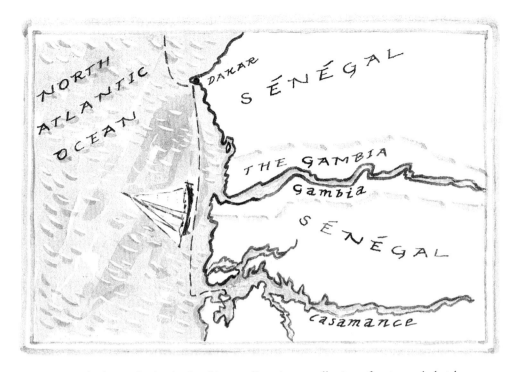

We had no pilot books for this coastline, just a collection of notes and sketches from fellow mariners.

I had just finished reading a book called *Tsotsi* by Athol Fugard about the lawlessness and anarchic, deadly violence of criminal gangs in South Africa and I was scared. Were we stepping into an horrific world beyond our understanding; where life was cheap; where law had broken down? It is a brilliant and deeply moral story, but I was wishing I hadn't read the damn thing quite so recently. I tried to get Magnus or Julia to read the book as well so that I could put my views into the wider context of theirs, but I had hung on to my dog-eared copy for so long that they had no interest in reading it just now. I should have read a bit of Joseph Conrad instead – he was certainly keen enough to expose man's frailties and inhumanity.

It helped enormously that my first impressions of Africa were French. They are the least threatening people in Europe, apart from their brutal motorcycle police. I love their reassuringly unthreatening greetings, with kisses, handshakes and, '*Ça va?*'. Even so, this touchy-feely French stuff was a little overdone when it nearly swamped the club launch taking us ashore after we moored. All the salty French yachties jumping on at the bow had to hurl themselves on the gnarled local boatman at the back to give him a thorough handshaking and kissing. On our second morning we were pressed into doing this ourselves when the gnarled local boatman gave us an emphatic '*Ça va?*' and a short lecture on social niceties. Everywhere, everyone, of all ages, diffused any social uncertainty with their '*Ça va?*'

Both Dakar yacht clubs, the CVD and the ADP, are a few miles east of the city, at Hann. The CVD is used by visitors while the ADP is where long-stay boats stop. We aimed for the CVD, but somehow ended up at the ADP and were welcomed. The sailors at the ADP are the naval equivalent of the unofficial French Foreign Legion. They are drawn to the wilder places of the earth and their talk is of out-of-the-way places in (mainly French-speaking) Africa and ocean crossings to empty parts of South America. By the time their stay has stretched from two weeks to two years, they know a lot about West Africa.

> **Hann anchorage**
> We followed the buoys from the white lighthouse on Cap Manuel at the end of the mainland, round Goree, across a well-buoyed bay to Pointe de Bel Air, conspicuous by its golden sandy beaches.
>
> The long breakwater on the east of the Pointe seemed to protect a military anchorage. Neither were shown on our photocopied charts and took us a bit by surprise. The picture became clearer when we saw yachts on moorings and pontoons of two yacht clubs. We anchored, but were immediately advised against this by a nearby yacht. The bottom is weedy and covered in rubbish. We picked up a free mooring buoy.

Dakar city, Senegal

Dakar city is hot and dusty, a modern Westernised city in a poor African country. It was not a place to restock. Supermarket prices were high. Imported foods were heavily taxed. Fresh fruit and vegetables in the street markets were good, but not as good or as cheap as in the Casamance.

Timing is important. The main depot of Senegal Gas, Segas, was out of propane on the days we went there to re-fill a bottle; then they closed for holidays. We left Dakar with one of our three gas bottles empty and no chance of a re-fill this side of the Atlantic.

Goree Island, Senegal

Goree Island, when we first sailed passed it, looked like an artists' colony. Pretty, colourful buildings, rocks of black and gold and red, a ruined fort on the near-vertical southern cliff. In reality, Goree was one of the main slave collection points on this coast from the fifteenth century to the nineteenth century. Millions of Africans in chains passed through warehouse prisons before being shipped to Europe and the Americas.

Now Goree is a UN World Heritage centre and not at all like a slaving hell-hole. The small, pretty harbour with eighteenth-century European houses around it, the grand squares with huge shady trees, impressive public buildings, and the much slower tempo than Dakar, make this a refuge for many new types of people.

A thousand people live on the island. Those on the fringes of Goree life live up the hill among huge fortifications built just before the First World War, when the Great Powers were still defending their colonies. We met Baas up there. Baas lived in an

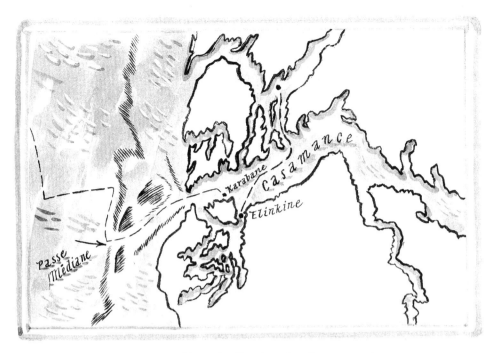

The Passe Médiane leading into the Casamance river.

ammunition room, under a huge gun emplacement. We wandered into his home by chance and he casually cadged a cigarette and chatted to us in his English, rather than our French. He explained his batik work then showed us round the little settlement on the hill, took us to a local restaurant we would never have found, introduced us to the cook, sorted out our order, cadged another cigarette, and left us to our meal.

The restaurant was in a long narrow cut, possibly originally a trench to link the gun emplacements or the wells, but now lush with passion fruit and papaya trees and well-tended vegetable rows. The man gardens; the woman cooks. The kitchen is a couple of fires: one for boiling and one for frying. The single table was in the shade of vines and trees. The food was good, but the fruit juice was wonderful. The passion fruit was picked as we watched. There was no bartering over price. Baas had told us the local price and that was all we were asked.

The full charm of the place on the hill came to us an hour later while having a cold beer in a waterfront bar in Goree, surrounded by hair braiders, bracelet sellers, shoe polishers, assorted beggars and a glut of tourists.

We anchored in sand just off the jetty where the ferry lands, and rowed ashore to the beach. I felt secure about the boat all the time we were ashore.

Casamance river

Our African sailing adventure was the River Casamance, 140 miles south of Dakar and 60 miles south of the Gambia. This is a low-lying coast of river deltas and mangrove shores. Gambia and the Casamance are large rivers, but south of them is the massive delta of Guinea-Bissau with its archipelago of islands. Offshore, even 10 or 15 miles, the sea is little more than 30 or 40 feet deep.

River entrance

Because passenger ships run between Ziguinchor and Dakar the buoys marking the entrance to the Casamance can be relied upon. We only half-believed it. We sighted the red and white outer fairway buoy on the third day out from Dakar, just as the wind was dying in mid-afternoon. The buoy was easy to spot. It was surrounded by a fleet of the largest and rustiest fishing hulks we had ever seen. They ploughed up and down the sea in lines, not a flake of paint on any of them.

The fairway buoy is about 10 miles offshore, due west of the river entrance. The coast is barely visible this far off. Five miles inshore of the buoy is the long river bar, cut by three channels with only the middle one buoyed. This, the Passe Médiane, was our target. The ebb tide runs hard and pilot instructions say only to enter two hours either side of high water. We didn't have a tidetable, and anyway all that is for big ships. They must take pilots. We didn't know how. Onshore winds break heavily on the bar and make the pass impossible. We were in luck that day.

We found the first of the buoys and dutifully ticked off the other reds and greens as the channel twisted south, then east, then south again. At times we seemed to be sailing away from the coast. As we ran due south along the 1 fathom edge of the bar, the waves reared up in the shallows. Farther in, on uncovering sand, they were breaking.

We needed number 8 red buoy, where Passe Médiane turns from south to northeast through a narrow cut in the sandbank. Then the course was simple: straight for the coast and the conspicuous light on Pointe de Djogue. Unfortunately the water along the bank was disturbed with no sign of a break in the bar.

We were motoring slowly south towards a tower we thought was number 8 buoy when we realised from the ever-shallowing water that we had lost the channel. We went back to number 6 buoy and from the comfort of deep water already visited, we saw number 8 up to the north-east, not to the south as shown on the chart. It was more or less on line to the Djogue light. After that, we came into the river without problem, watching white waves breaking on the inner shoals despite hardly a breeze blowing.

We came up close to the high light tower at Pointe de Djogue and hugged the shore until we were off the fishing village there. A pretty sight, of brightly painted pirogues drawn up on shore and fires amid thatched huts. The smell of drying fish was less attractive. We could see the acre of wires on which fish were laid out to dry. We could imagine the universe of fly-life over them. After the village we crossed the river to find an anchorage off the village of Karabane on Karabane Island. We passed between two horses in the river[1] and hoped that the huge black river dolphin swimming with us preferred deep water to rubbing their bellies on

---

[1]This horse is a sand or mud bank that rose as an obstruction in a channel.

muddy bottoms. They were our pilots. We anchored in 15 feet, just where the depth shoaled. Any closer in and we would have dried out just after high tide.

Karabane, Casamance

Karabane is a small friendly village with two restaurants and two shops. We were lucky, we bought some two-day-old bread from one of the shops. The next day we bought some three-day-old bread. We ate at the larger of the restaurants, sited in an old colonial-style mission house, a reminder that Karabane was once the capital of the Casamance. Dennis, an American, was restoring the old building. He hoped to bring in weekend visitors from Dakar now that the ferries were running. The food at Dennis's place was excellent. The beer was cold. Pity about the water. We were on our second jug when Dennis reappeared. It took him a second or two to realise what we were doing and then he grabbed the jug as if it contained poison.

'Even the locals don't drink that,' he told us. 'It probably isn't even safe to wash in.'

The old building has a tank to collect rainwater. The stuff is probably safe to drink during the wet season when it is fresh, but this was the dry season and that water had been standing for months, uncovered.

Dennis looked so worried for us that we tried to cheer him up. He was probably afraid that his first customers that month would die before they could come back a second time. We drank more beer, to stimulate the stomach enzymes that would save us. When the crew went dancing at a wedding celebration, invited by one of the waiters, I went back on board to stoically drink strong alcohol and save my stomach.

Karabane village is spread out under huge trees along streets of hardened earth. It is neat and tidy. Houses of wood and cane with thatched roofs. Low stockade fences to keep the chickens and children in and the pigs out.

Walking around the village we excited some interest and would have attracted more but the wedding celebrations were still in full flood. A great crowd of people were watching and taking part in the strangest event. Three women lined up, one of whom was the bride, to race through a clothes-washing ceremony. A pile of clothes had to be dipped, item by item, into washing water, rinsing water, and then flung into the hanging-out-to-dry pile. It was cursory and symbolic, wetting anyone within 20 feet of the bowls. It was surely rigged so that the bride would win. Pity, then, that a very competitive lady hadn't been told the rules.

After the race came the dance. Each woman did an energetic knees-up and then kicked dust into the bride's face. The point seemed to be to goad the poor, glum-faced woman into retaliation because the moment came when she could bear this no longer. She jumped up and did her own wild knees-up and kicked dirt. She still looked fairly glum.

Meanwhile, a pig was turned slowly on a spit over an open fire. We could have been the first white people ever to attend a bridal ceremony at Karabane. Small children came over just to touch us and quietly hold our hand for a few seconds. Then they ran away and giggled with their friends.

This was the Dark Continent of Conrad and Lord Jim, where the last traces of European colonialism were rotting under the encroaching bush. The old Africa of mud huts and huge shade trees to save its people from the burning sun. The remote Africa where children had never touched a white person before. And in this old Africa two locals in front of us were camcording the whole event, and most male teenagers wore tee-shirts from American universities. We were probably the only people in the crowd who didn't have a shower, television and cold beer waiting at home.

Elinkine, Casamance

Elinkine is larger and poorer than Karabane, but the bread is one day nearer the bakery and therefore fresher. We went back down the Casamance until we could enter the Marigot d'Elinkine and take this creek around the island of Karabane. We saw one other yacht, anchored under trees in a lonely and beautiful spot, some fishing huts, and small, crude jetties. At one jetty close to the razor-wired Club Med resort at Cap Skiring, white tourists clambered with difficulty into a pirogue. They were going sightseeing. They soon passed us at high speed, their white faces just a shade paler with fear of capsize. We waved, as we waved to all pirogues on the river. Unlike every other pirogue, no one waved back. White-knuckled hands gripped the gunwales of the pirogue.

Elinkine village is the junction between road and river. It has a petrol station, tourist centre, and little shops and market stalls under the baobab tree down by the landing place. It has water, but the tap is slow and the queue long. The anchorage is noisy and smelly. The fish laid out to dry on reeds cover about 500 yards, and in turn are covered by flies. Pirogues go by continuously, outboards at full throttle. Everyone seemed welcoming but we preferred Karabane. The flies were more than we could take. Our high spot was a deserted hamlet of tourist huts with a working shower.

The next morning we ran aground when misguided by a green navigation buoy. This either marked a very narrow deep-water channel close to the Karabane shore, or was well out of position. We were very suspicious but not enough. We were discussing untrustworthy buoys when we lost depth in mid-river and hit mud. We had no bottom on one side of the boat and 3 feet on the other. We tried reversing and kedging but we were stuck.

We waited patiently for the tide to turn and rowed two anchors out fore-and-aft, not being sure which way we would come off. After a while a nasty little wind with its nasty little wavelets started pushing us up the mud-bank. We were heeled over into 3 feet of water with worryingly little idea of tide times and heights. As we began to appreciate that this wind could drive us up the horse all the way to high tide, and then leave us there, we became more active in refloating. We wound both anchor lines tight. Then we waited a bit. Then we tried a bit of engine in reverse. Then we waited a bit. Then we tried a bit of engine ahead. Then we wound the anchor lines tighter. Then we tried all this but with shorter periods of waiting. Finally we gambled on getting rid of one of the anchor lines since we seemed to

Rush hour on the strand at Karabane.

be nearly afloat but trapped by the combined forces of the fore-and-aft anchors and the wind on the beam. We planned a finger-risking operation to let go the bow line, slam on reverse engine, and haul like hell on the stern anchor. We slid slowly off the mud. Magnus, whose brute strength had mainly got us off the mud, was encouraged to row off and recover the bow anchor while Julia and I motored slowly around in deep water. I was more worried than I would admit to at the time.

Adventure in the bush

After the Marigot d'Elinkine we thought the narrow Bolon Ouniomoueye looked an adventurous place to enter. We grounded twice on the mudflats before we got anywhere near the dried-out Bolon, so we gave up and headed for the much wider and easier Marigot de Gambie. The Casamance at this point is about 3 miles wide, but the low mangroves make it look wider. Where we were, on a great bend in the river, the far shore was 7 or 8 miles away.

The Marigot de Gambie leads eventually into the River Gambia or back to the Atlantic through one of the many smaller rivers. We went 5 miles then turned into a narrow, tree-lined section of the Kalisseye river, and anchored. The Marigot de Gambie was a mile across at this point and our little river about 200 yards wide. At the ocean, the Kalisseye is 3 miles wide, but made impassable by sandbanks.

We had a wonderfully remote and peaceful anchorage for the evening. We rowed ashore to investigate and immediately started jumping at shadows. We city kids did not know what was in this wild part of Africa. The large paw marks might be lions or tigers. Strange tracks on the dried earth reminded us of crocodiles, rustles in the reeds might be snakes. Surely no human had set foot here before?

It turned out that we were walking along the edge of rice paddies that a nearby village cultivated in the wet season. In the dry season villagers came only to fish. We met a small group of young men laying fish out to dry. They asked, in French, what we were doing, and we replied, in French, that we were taking a promenade. They looked at us in pity, either at our French or our promenading, then one asked if we would like to visit his house and meet his father. He probably thought we needed entertainment. We wondered if this was a trap for unwary foreigners.

We were led across dried-up paddies towards a distant clump of huge trees, trying to make friendly conversation in French as we went. The young man leading us said many things in excellent French, few of which we could understand. The two men behind us merely smiled. I think they could see how ignorant we were. We learnt that they were brothers. As we neared the trees we saw lean-to buildings and two men sitting on the ground. A small child was playing, some chickens ran about. We had no idea where we were.

One of the men under the trees was our guide's father. The other was his grandfather. Both were very pleased to meet us and began offering us food and drink. One son went to get palm wine, another climbed a huge tree to get *pain de chenge*, a fruit we called monkey bread. The father switched off the radio, which had been broadcasting in French. They were forgiving of our execrable French. The father said his English was just as bad, and then shamed us with a perfect sentence. Like

We met a group of young men laying out fish to dry; they took us to meet their father and grandfather.

his sons, he had learnt English at school and was interested in events in Britain. What did we think of John Major and Margaret Thatcher? The politics of neither were approved. Here, under these shade trees, in their ragged shorts and shirts, with the chickens and pigs running around in the dirt, the world's news arrived and was chewed over just as much as in London or New York. We had barely listened to radio news for a month. I knew that our superior Marks & Spencer clothing could not save us when the father turned to Julia, now identified as American not British, and asked about President Clinton. Her lack of French saved the day.

We faced and fought a number of ignorant presumptions that day. All of them our own. Magnus described Dakar to one of the raggedy sons and asked if he had ever been there. 'Oh yes. I took a degree in agriculture there and came back here to practise it.'

As we sat, other fishermen came by and stopped to talk — rough-looking sons of toil. Strong men, with bands around their biceps that displayed their muscles threateningly, wore sweat-stained work-clothes. Each without exception said 'Ça va' and shook hands all round. Each was particularly courteous to us, the foreign guests.

133

Magnus – trying not to tip the pirogue.

The father and son walked us to the river and came on board to look at *Petronella*. The boat was a new world for them. They were curious about everything. They seemed to know as much about the technology of GPS as we did. Next day they came back in a pirogue with a shotgun. The son took Magnus and Julia hunting while we two old men reclined in the saloon and discussed the world, our beliefs, and what motivated us.

Ziguinchor, Casamance
Ziguinchor, the main town on the river, was always with us. The bridge is as far as masted boats can get. People on the river marked our journey by when we would arrive and leave Ziguinchor. It is a town of some charm and bustle, with good markets and shops. It was taken for granted that we would enjoy ourselves there.

Pirogues move continuously on Ziguinchor waterfront. We anchored off the Parroquet bar and restaurant, where most yachts anchor and crews get ashore over the restaurant fence at all states of the tide and at all states of business in the restaurant without anyone objecting. We filled our water containers for free at the bar, but made a point of buying beer and coffee there.

The holding is good in thick mud but the river narrows to 200 yards here, the channel is 30 feet deep, currents are strong, and the wind sometimes blows force 4 downriver. Anchored yachts slalom all over the place.

We enjoyed some local life through Alain and Antionette from Dakar as soon as we reached Ziguinchor. We went to Antionette's seven-day-old niece's name-day feast. As the feast wore on we became part of the children's favourite game: touch a white person. The game was great fun for us because we didn't have to be good at it. If we turned to grab the child just as they were reaching to touch us they would scream with horror, their eyes opening wide, and then dash back to the safety of their friends and giggle hysterically.

Bye - bye Ziguinchor
We left Ziguinchor on New Year's Day, the last of the flood tide against us, a good wind behind us, and the groans of some French revellers in our ears after we banged on their steel hull. *Zout alors*, they had banged on ours at dawn three hours earlier.

When the wind died we motored in a baking 32°C. Tiny flies stuck to us and we wondered about using the Elinkine beach shower. The GPS said 31 miles to Karabane, 2600 to Tobago.

Going downriver we saw old acquaintances from Porto Santo. We drifted, chatting together in mid-stream while they wished us a safe journey, then we went on to the ocean and they headed upstream to Ziguinchor.

Leaving the river

On 2 January in the river mouth a light onshore wind against tide raised white water all along the sand bars. Breaking waves blocked the channel at number 8 red buoy 2 miles offshore, where we had made our little error coming into the Casamance. We guessed that the channel took a major dog-leg turn here, where the river had cut through the hard sand of the long bar. The narrow cut would run around the steep end of one sandbank and across the shallow tail of another. The waves were occasionally as high as 8 to 10 feet and breaking frequently. Big enough to flip us over backwards or bury our bows. The channel was barred to us.

Short waves broke continuously on the mud to starboard so we eased across to port. Our depth dropped and fluctuated by 6 feet as the swells came under us, but this was less threatening with fewer breakers. We bolted the forehatch, put washboards in, revved up the engine, and crossed our fingers. We were lucky. The worst breakers were inside us and we slipped around with just a few lumpy seas to soak us.

Once out of the main channel we did not bother with the clear water buoy to our north. We were outside the banks. We sheeted tight and headed west for the Caribbean. Less than 2600 miles to go.

Africa: a closing comment

This is not the coast for a three-week visit. This is not the Canaries, with the familiarities of Europe mediated through islands and sunshine. This is the edge of a wholly foreign continent. It deserves months or years. At the very least we should have come sooner and left later. We came by chance, an unplanned excursion. It was easy. We picked up charts and guides for the price of the photocopying. The best advice of all was to go to Dakar and ask the sailors there which rivers to visit.

The Casamance was wonderful at that time of year. It is a large river by European standards, with islands and tributaries to explore, and the people of its isolated villages travel by pirogue rather than road.

We had short, lazy days on the river. It was chilly till about nine in the morning, so we didn't stir before then. We anchored at dusk, about seven in the evening. We used the mornings, when the tide was ebbing, to go ashore and explore. After midday we took the rising tide upriver, sailing whenever the wind allowed. Sometimes we found villages to visit, mostly we just pulled out of the current in some pretty spot and anchored. Nothing much moved on the river after dark and certainly not us. We needed daylight to navigate the mudbanks that in places might be a mile off the shore. Buoys mark the main channel but none are lit. Nor are the fish floats or the pirogues.

The drum we bought came complete with a lesson on how to play it.

We enjoyed the natural life of the river even in our deep ignorance. There were huge, wonderful trees, new to me. I wished for a book on birds. We saw a whole range of heron–like birds, some with a wingspan of at least 6 feet, others pure white, others deep blue with yellow feet. We saw pelican, eagles, vultures and beautiful brightly coloured smaller birds.

The river was full of fish, which we seldom saw, and huge black river dolphins which we saw everywhere. They were never as easy to see in the murky water as dolphins at sea but they made up for this by swimming close to us and taking longer on the surface to breathe. Slow, lazy, powerful swimmers.

The people were, of course, just as fascinating. A medieval lifestyle in touch with modern technology, polite French manners with an African warmth. I do not know how many visiting yachts have this close experience of Africa. We were lucky and very privileged.

If only we had had more time. We didn't leave Africa because we wanted to, but because our destination was the Caribbean. I spent half the crossing wondering how to return to Africa. By this time I had realised that I had sailed enough around north-west Europe. Sailing in the south was what I wanted. I figured that sailing to Africa from Europe needn't be the same commitment as an Atlantic crossing.

Paradise

Two popular arrival points in the Caribbean are Barbados and the middle islands of the chain such as St Lucia or Antigua. We didn't choose Barbados because some remarks in the pilot book put us off. Now I may never go there because it is so hard to travel that far east out of the main line of islands. If you want to visit Barbados, go there first.

St Lucia is one of the most beautiful islands in the chain with good harbours and welcoming facilities. A lot of British yachts are based there. Antigua has one of the most memorable and safe harbours in this part of the island chain in English Harbour/Nelson's Dockyard. Sailing into this is like sailing into the eighteenth century. The advantage of arriving in the middle of the chain is that you have the winds to command the rest of the islands. You can go north or south without hard beating.

Instead we chose Trinidad & Tobago. We were already a long way south for our departure, so it seemed sensible to aim at the southern end of the Caribbean. There are no complications about reaching either Trinidad or Tobago, as there are if you approach across the reefy archipelago between Grenada and St Vincent. And if we followed the plan of coming back six months later, we could see all the Caribbean simply by going north up the chain as we would have to anyway. Any other landing would mean doubling back or missing sections.

Having got to Trinidad & Tobago we discovered yet another reason for arriving here first. Tobago is certainly one of the most beautiful islands in the whole Caribbean and probably the least spoilt. It has everything that even the most fevered imagination could think of under the title Caribbean Paradise. Trinidad is a large and industrial island, although you need never be aware of this, and as such has better repair and fitting-out facilities than the smaller islands. Trinidad has a large community of long-stay cruisers, mainly American, and their well-organised VHF radio net eases you into life there. Also, the cost of living in Trinidad & Tobago is roughly half that in the rest of the Caribbean.

Log entry: entering Paradise
We call it Paradise. The locals call it Trinidad & Tobago. After 22 days we've arrived and it's the most wonderful thing in the world. The anchorage in Scarborough is a bit rolly but we don't even notice it. We've been racing against the clock all day. We lost and won, together. We knew this morning that we would make Scarborough by dark, so that wasn't the problem. The race was against the customs and immigration overtime charges after 4 pm.

The strong morning wind fell away in the afternoon and we motored to keep up speed. We have done four hours' motoring in the last 22 days. The very last four hours.

Trinidad & Tobago
Tobago came up as a dark smudge under white clouds when we were less than 20 miles away. Even if there was treasure awaiting us in Trinidad we wouldn't have been able to resist the lure of the first land sighted after three weeks at sea. Now, as though time mattered after so long at sea, we were desperate to make land.

From 10 miles we saw Tobago as a clear outline, but not well enough to make out Scarborough, our port of entry. At 5 miles the land became beautifully green and wooded and the houses grander. We corkscrewed in on 10 foot waves and a 2 knot current with the wind a disappointingly light easterly 4. We carried full sail past the rocky breakwater and anchored behind two other boats in 25 feet.

Geoffrey was cooking lunch that day.

At 1620 I met two immigration officials on their way home. When they said we had to put out to sea if I did not pay the overtime charge, I thought of what the crew would do to me and paid the US$20 fee. I was no sooner back on *Petronella* when a large man swam out from the Coast Guard hut on the break-water. Tony, the senior Coast Guard, wanted to ask about our journey and tell us about his island. I can't think of any other Coast Guard chief who would have taken the trouble, but we soon found that Tony was not the only charming Tobagonian. We wandered into Kim's bar that evening to be greeted by Kim, his wife and all the customers there. They take 'liming' seriously. (This was the first time we had heard the word. Liming is the art of socialising for the sake of it, and it is a high art form in Tobago.) By the time the evening finished we had been fed roti and dhal and given stuff to take for breakfast, and the most unlikely Rastafarian with an accent we barely understood was bringing bread-fruit, coconut, herbs and spices to cook for us the next day. Geoffrey. We were to spend a lot of time with Geoffrey. No wonder we thought we had arrived in Paradise. Food, drink, friends, and no trade wind sailing.

Tobago is not to be rushed. Allow more time that you anticipated. The place is not crowded with yachts because it is just that little bit too difficult to get to from most places except the Atlantic Ocean.

Scarborough, Tobago

Come in on the buoyed channel, turn the breakwater, and swing back along it to anchor as close as feels comfortable and as far in from the entrance as possible.

Scarborough has good shops and services. Stock up. You will find nothing in the little villages beyond rum shops and fruit and vegetables, except for Store Bay where the airport and most of the hotels are. Apart from Scarborough, Tobago is an island of beach and bay anchorages.

Store Bay, Tobago

Store Bay is the first stop for most boats after Scarborough and only an hour or so around the south corner of the island. It has a beautiful beach and excellent local food by the bar. Take shore clothes in a bin-liner in case the surf rolls your dinghy. If the surf is really bad, go on a mile to a gut-way in the south-west end of Bacco reef. Thirty feet of water, reef either side, well protected, but a long row ashore to Crown Point, everyone's idea of a Caribbean beach.

Englishman's Bay, Tobago

The most beautiful bay and very quiet. This is a turtle-egg-laying beach. The sand is coarse and the beach shelves steeply to give a second tier above high water. That is what leatherbacks like. The heavy surf is a problem when waves are smashing at this steep shelf.

Patches of bright orange immortelle trees in flower, noisy green parrots flying home, and then the flickering of a million fireflies.

Charlottesville, Tobago

If the surf is up, go straight to Charlottesville, the prettiest town on the island. The anchorage in Pirate's Bay is calm and quiet but an easy row to town. Landing by dinghy at the town jetty is easy.

The unspoilt beauty of Englishman's Bay, Tobago. Its most frequent visitors are the leatherback turtles — for egg-laying purposes.

Take a walk in the rainforest from here. Use a knowledgeable guide. I can follow a footpath as well as any taxi driver, but that is not the point when visiting a rainforest. The forest on Tobago (and Trinidad) is as rich in species as those of South America. You need a well-informed naturalist, not a taxi driver, to tell you about this, and an experienced guide to spot the birds and mammals, never mind know their names.

Parlatuvia, Tobago
A pretty bay with a tiny village and fleet of small fishing boats. Three yachts fill this anchorage. The entrance is narrow and easier to spot from the south than the north. The pilot says it has less surf than other bays, but we were glad to move on.

Tobago to Trinidad: through the Dragon's Mouth
A fast boat could make this trip in daylight. We went overnight and had to wait for dawn. There are three entrances, or *boccas*, to the Gulf of Paria. The trade wind current rushing past these *boccas* creates rough water as far as 2 miles offshore, depending on the wind strength. The first *bocca* is the nearest to Tobago, but I prefer the second. It has a wider entrance, no nasty rock in the middle, and can be sailed through.

Chaguaramas, Trinidad
Chaguaramas is probably the yachting centre of the eastern Caribbean. Turn east out of the *boccas* and Chaguaramas is where all the yachts are anchored. All the yards have good places to eat and drink and a good social life. Start by listening to the cruisers' radio net on channel 68 at 8 am each morning.

Take care anchoring here. Yachts swing unpredictably in the afternoon. Don't leave the boat until you know how close you swing to your neighbours.

Is that it?

◆ *This is not a journey that ends. This is something that defines your life.*
◆ *Don't make too much of a meal of the plans and preparations. The point is to make sure you get started. After that, go where the wind blows you.*

I'm not going home yet

Another dark tropical evening. The air was warm and I could smell new paint as I sat in the cockpit of *Nellie Matilda*, back against the mizzen mast, while Rick and Bill picked up the thread of an earlier discussion. The meaning of life seemed to be in there somewhere, along with the trials and tribulations of a sailing life and whether Bill should have read *Catcher in the Rye* when he was a teenager in Australia, rather than now when he was pushing early middle age in the Caribbean. Personally, I was marvelling at having a cold beer without going to a bar. *Nellie Matilda* has a fridge, *and* it was working. *Petronella* has beer in the bilge, but not a chilling breeze anywhere.

Bill's boat was about 20 feet off the quarter of *Nellie Matilda*. I had just been hearing about when he built it and why, and how well it had sailed all the way up the coast of South America. Now he has a partner, it is too small, and he feels he should move up from a home-made 28 footer with a 12 foot bowsprit and back addition that looked like a country dunny, to a classic 80 footer with more luxury than a swagman could shake a stick at. I looked across at his little boat. She looked fine to me. With her bows pointed straight at us, I could only see her elegance. It made me forget the 'porta-loo' on the stern.

I couldn't see *Petronella* from where I sat, far down in this deep cockpit. But I knew exactly where she was: 200 yards away. Next door was *Orion* and not much farther on was *Sisi*, close companions since we met in Tobago six weeks before. *Nellie Matilda*, of course, I had known since we met her in Gijon after crossing Biscay, and then at various points in our journey since. She was already ashore at Chaguaramas when we sailed into Trinidad.

Orion, *Sisi* and *Petronella* will be left ashore for the next six months. *Nellie Matilda* launches soon. Magnus is living aboard her and helping Rick with the work before going to California to join Julia.

I looked up at the night sky, duller here with so much background light from the land, and let the conversation drift by. I shall be home in a few days. Time for me to earn a living again. I am looking forward to the change. I have had enough of boating for the time being and want the challenges of work and the pleasure of seeing family and friends. My head mixes thoughts of home with the jobs needed to make *Petronella* fit to survive months in the tropics. I am thinking of Carnival, now reaching its finale here, and the films and books I will find back in London. It is a good mix, with very few flies in the ointment just now.

And what about you?

So we made it. Crossing the ocean in a small boat is a life-defining event. If you have even the slightest feeling that you could do it, do it. No ocean crossing should be undertaken lightly and no crossing is worth less than any other. So prepare carefully, take the Milk Run, and let it give your life a new definition.

The pedantic and ungenerous who have read this far will be grumbling that I have only written half a book. I got you to the Caribbean, but what happens next? Oh, come on, I told you at the beginning that my plans for the return-half got binned and I'm still enjoying sailing trips here. I can assure you that if you get as far as the Caribbean you will know what to do next, but the choices are so great that I can't possibly suggest which one will suit you best. I mean, how can I forecast your next step when I couldn't even forecast my own?

You might still be following the plans you made before you left home, or which you firmed up on the way. More likely, you will have been winging it for the last three months and got used to an uncertain tomorrow. Now you can head north to visit the USA and all those American crews who gave you their addresses. Or you can head for the Azores and go north for home or south to Africa. Or there is Panama and the Pacific. Or you can wrap the boat in cotton wool and send her home deck cargo while you enjoy one of the supreme pleasures of having taken 20 to 30 days to sail the Atlantic Ocean: flying home in seven hours.

Appendices

Appendix 1: *Petronella*: the boat

Petronella is a C–Mist 32 designed by Samson Marine of Canada and built in Oban, Scotland, by her original owners and launched in 1979. She is a double–ended–type yacht with a Bermudan cutter rig.

Dimensions and specification
LOA on deck: 9.9m (32ft 2in)
LWL: 8.03m (27ft 6in)
Beam: 3.43m (11ft 2in)
Draft: 1.54m (5ft)
Displacement: 9.5 tonnes (Atlantic cruising weight about 11 tonnes)
Headroom: 0.3m (6ft)
Bowsprit: 1m (3ft 6in)
Mast: 12.8m (42ft)
Engine: Bukh 20hp
Diesel fuel capacity: 30 Imperial gallons (136 litres) in two fitted tanks; the same in plastic containers
Water capacity: 45 Imperial gallons (204 litres) in three fitted tanks; another 30 gallons (136 litres) in plastic containers

Petronella is rigged for convenient singlehanding. Her stable hull and roomy deck make a safe working platform at sea. Her long keel gives directional stability and a great sense of security in bad weather. Her rigging and deck gear is more rugged and strong than on most cruising yachts of her length; her ferro-cement construction is immensely strong.

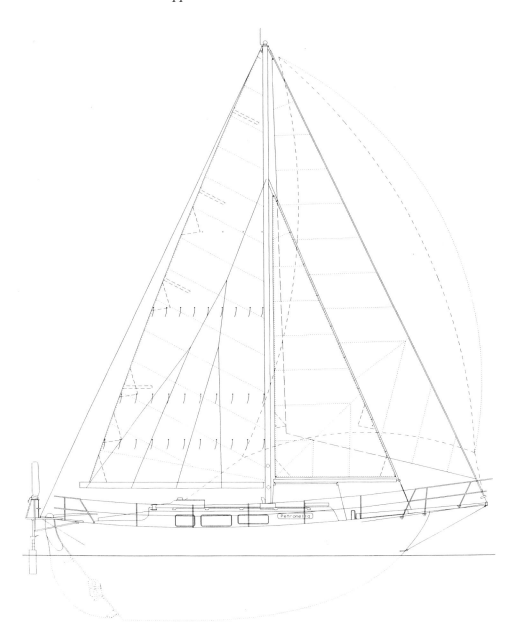

Layout

Internal layout, going forward

Galley and navigation area: Galley to starboard and full-sized chart table to port; main water tank under floor.

Engine compartment: Aft of galley.

Saloon: Four berths, good grab-handles, paraffin lamps on bulkheads; water tanks and spare anchors under floor.

Toilet: Baby Blake sea-toilet.

Cockpit: Self-draining. Lockers port, starboard and aft.

Forecabin: Two single berths; tool and chain locker.

Forepeak: Sail etc stowage.

Petronella was well equipped but not lavishly so. Life was not a continual mainte-nance chore. She carried GPS, VHF, EPIRB, echo sounder, steering compass, tel-tale compass below, trailing log, two manual bilge pumps, and one electric with automatic switching, at least four fire extinguishers and two fire blankets, a full set of emergency flares. All berths have lee cloths.

The Avon 2.4m (8ft) inflatable was rowed with all three of us on board and lug-gage. We had no outboard engine. We hired a four-person Ocean standard liferaft in a valise which was stored below. The first emergency in abandoning ship would have been the medical one of a hernia induced by hoisting this raft up to the cockpit.

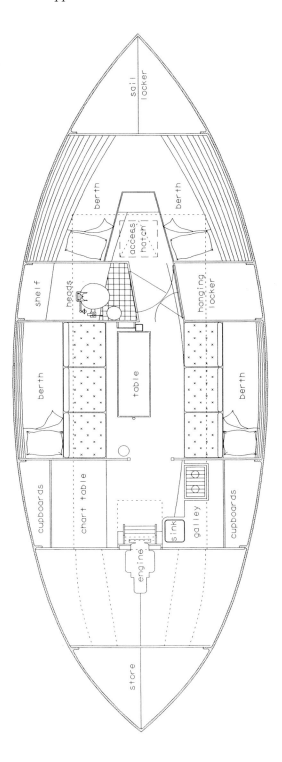

Sails, steering and ground tackle

Sails: *Main:* 29.7sq m (320sq ft) four slab reefs.

Roller furling: MPG 41.8sq m (450sq ft); genoa 27.8sq m (300sq ft); jibs 13.9sq m (150sq ft).

Cruising chute: 46.4sq m (500sq ft) with snuffer and sock.

Staysails: 9.2sq m (100sq ft), boomed self-tacking with reefing points.

Storm trysail.

Rudder: Massive barn-door-type rudder, tiller about 1.8m (6ft) long.

Anchors: *Main:* 15kg (33lb) Bruce on 54.8m (180ft) $^3/_8$ in (10mm) chain

Spares: 12.2kg (27lb) Fishermans

13.6kg (30lb) Danforth

20.4kg (45lb) Brittany-type

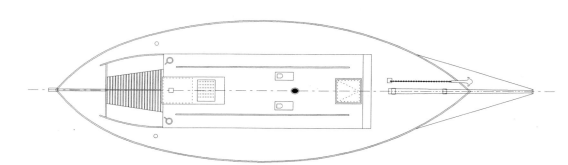

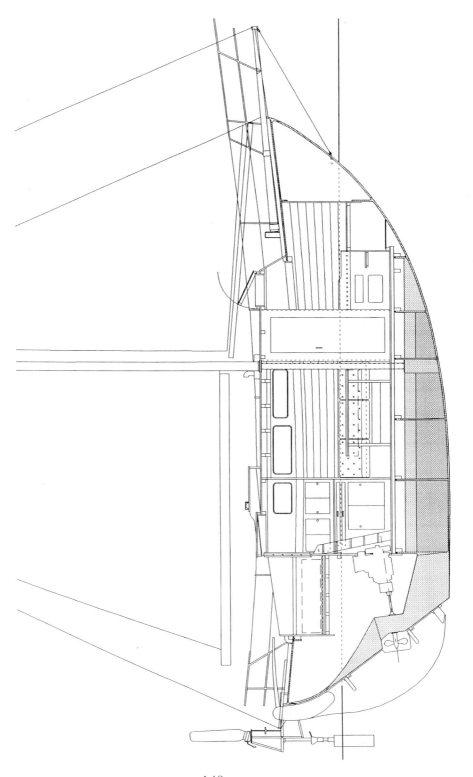

Appendix 2: References

Rogue Storm – a true story of disaster and survival in a force 12 storm in the Pacific by Tony Harrington. Read it to show what boats can really survive. Published by Waterline 1996.

Sailing writers to look out for:

Caldwell, John The most astonishing story of a sailing novice who took on an ocean and survived. Just. Even the crew of *Petronella* took inspiration from *Desperate Voyage*, Adlard Coles Nautical.

Chichester, Francis Read him to see what a singlehander can do.

Coles, Adlard The man to read about coping with storms at sea: *Heavy Weather Sailing*, Adlard Coles Nautical.

Hiscocks, Eric and Susan The doyens of blue water sailing. Read any of their books for information and inspiration.

Jones, Tristan A prolific author who writes about his idiosyncratic sailing adventures.

Moitessier, Bernard French sailing hero and guru. Read him for information and inspiration, starting with his account of sailing round Cape Horn, *Cape Horn: The Logical Route* Published by Grafton Books.

O'Brien, Connor Tremendous trip across the Pacific and round Cape Horn.

Rose, Sir Alec He gives a fascinating account of racing singlehanded across the Atlantica in *My Lively Lady*, Adlard Coles Nautical.

Slocum, Joshua The man who provided inspiration, singlehanding around the world recounted in his book *Sailing Alone Around the World*, Adlard Coles Nautical.

Smeeton, Miles and Beryl Lots to choose from. Start with their account of being pitch-poled on the way to Cape Horn, *Once is Enough* Published by Grafton Books.

Tilman, William Phlegmatic sailor and climber – unmatched and unmatchable. His crew seldom seemed to reach his standards, however.

Index